T0216364

Lecture Notes in Computer Science 9400

Commenced Publication in 1973
Founding and Former Series Editors:
Gerhard Goos, Juris Hartmanis, and Jan van Leeuwen

More information about this series at http://www.springer.com/series/7408

Betty H.C. Cheng · Benoit Combemale
Robert B. France · Jean-Marc Jézéquel
Bernhard Rumpe (Eds.)

Globalizing Domain-Specific Languages

International Dagstuhl Seminar
Dagstuhl Castle, Germany, October 5–10, 2014
Revised Papers

 Springer

Editors

Betty H.C. Cheng
Michigan State University
East Lansing, MI
USA

Jean-Marc Jézéquel
IRISA, Université de Rennes 1
Rennes
France

Benoit Combemale
IRISA, Université de Rennes 1
Rennes
France

Bernhard Rumpe
RWTH Aachen University
Aachen
Germany

Robert B. France (†)
Colorado State University
Fort Collins, CO
USA

ISSN 0302-9743   ISSN 1611-3349   (electronic)
Lecture Notes in Computer Science
ISBN 978-3-319-26171-3   ISBN 978-3-319-26172-0   (eBook)
DOI 10.1007/978-3-319-26172-0

Library of Congress Control Number: 2015953257

LNCS Sublibrary: SL2 – Programming and Software Engineering

Springer Cham Heidelberg New York Dordrecht London

Printed on acid-free paper

Springer International Publishing AG Switzerland is part of Springer Science+Business Media
(www.springer.com)

Foreword

Dismantling the "Tower of Babel"

The design and construction of complex technical systems such as cyber-physical systems has always been a difficult process due to the sheer number and diversity of design decisions that need to be made. What makes this particularly challenging is the fact that many of these design choices are interdependent, so that selecting a particular alternative constrains the choices available for other decisions. This issue is becoming more vexing as the number of potential technical alternatives increases with technical progress while, at the same time, there is an ever-growing demand for more sophisticated system functionality. To make this intricate task manageable, engineers have throughout history relied on the trusted "divide and conquer" technique; that is, first decomposing a complex problem to be solved into more manageable sub-problems, then solving each of them individually, and, finally, combining the resulting solutions into a single integrated system. Depending on the size and complexity of the system under consideration, the same approach may have to be applied at multiple hierarchically nested levels.

A fundamental weakness of this approach is that any decomposition of the original problem is itself a critical design choice that invariably has repercussions on many key downstream design decisions. Exacerbating this is the fact that the decomposition decision has to be made early, when least is known about the problem and possible solutions. Consequently, it is not uncommon to see that, as development progresses and problem understanding grows, engineers begin to realize that their chosen decomposition is suboptimal and that others would have been more suitable. Unfortunately, all too often this realization comes too late because significant time, resources, and effort may have already been expended developing the system based on the original decomposition, meaning that any major re-engineering would be either impractical or prohibitively expensive.

To minimize the risk of inappropriate decompositions, it is necessary for the design and development teams to gain insight and experience with the problem on hand as early as possible. Clearly, since the system to be developed does not exist until it is implemented, another age-old engineering technique is used: the use of models to represent the intended design of components yet to be built. These engineering models can take many different forms, including renderings that only exist as ideas in designers heads. However, to be truly useful, an engineering model must take on a concrete form so that it can be communicated to other stakeholders as well as analyzed for suitability. Formal models in particular are desirable since they can be analyzed by formal (i.e., mathematical or logical) means, which, if the analyses are conducted correctly, are more likely to yield correct and, hence, more trustworthy results. Moreover, if the models are realized on a computer, many of the mechanistic aspects of the analysis procedure can be automated.

While computer-based models can help provide more trustworthy analysis results, they do not on their own solve the problem of design decision inter-dependencies unless, of course, the models themselves are linked in appropriate ways. How to link models, particularly models of different subsystems, is one of the primary themes of this volume. Until we had computer-based subsystem models, the only way to link models was through textual reference or human recall methods that have proven highly error prone at best. With the use of computer-supported hyperlinking it is possible to make such links not only more reliable but, even more importantly, more meaningful. This is because it is possible for them to account in various ways for the specific semantics of the model elements that are being linked. Thus, a hyperlink between a software component in a model of the software and an element representing a processor in a model of the intended hardware platform can be customized to capture the specific nature of the software deployment relationship. With that information it might be possible, for example, to compute whether or not the processor is sufficiently powerful to support that software component.

But, even with such computer-aided support, one major problem remains: what if the models whose elements are to be linked are specified using different modeling languages? This is much more than just a syntactical issue: different modeling languages may be based on very different semantic foundations. For example, time in one language may be modeled as a continuous quantity whereas it may be discrete in another. Or, one language may be used to model software while another represents the thermal aspects of a system – two radically different domains based on very different paradigms and different ontologies. Yet, although the various languages used in the design of a complex system deal with different phenomena, they all describe components of the same system, including some that are simultaneously present in multiple models but in different forms.

How should this heterogeneity of paradigms and languages be handled? What is the nature of these "semantically aware" hyperlinks? The salient approaches proposed here may come as a surprise to some, particularly given the use of the term "globalization", which might in the minds of some people connote an Esperanto-like homogenization and unification. What we see, instead, is a more subtle and a much more pragmatic approach based on integration rather than replacement. Even a superficial analysis on how much has been invested in existing technologies and languages reveals that it would be impractical to replace them with some new "universal" language and toolset combination – even if we could realistically devise one. The history of technological progress teaches us that most viable technical disciplines are constantly evolving, sprouting new offshoots (i.e., new sub-disciplines) along the way. Each of these is a specialization of another specialization, all of it driven by the need to reason concisely and yet accurately about domain-specific concerns and phenomena. This leads to an ever-increasing number of domain-specific modeling paradigms and languages. Without doubt, this trend will never cease. Consequently, "globalization" as used in this volume means co-existence, and more specifically, collaboration at the system level.

Needless to say, such solutions to this "Tower of Babel" syndrome are not new, yet we have failed to deal with it effectively in the past. So, what has changed to give us hope that we finally have a realistic crack at overcoming it now? It is my conjecture that this is mostly due to the recent emergence of (or, more precisely, the beginnings of) a general theory of modeling languages. This was prompted by the standardization of a few key modeling languages including notably UML and SysML. While neither of these can be held up as a paragon of technical perfection, their very flaws (ambiguity, redundancy, lack of precision, etc.) inspired a strong research movement to understand how they can be improved. This seems to have provided the necessary catalyst, which, combined with other recent technological advances, such as ever more powerful computing and communications systems and new generations of computer-based tools, has created the basis for radically new ways of engineering complex technical systems. That is, when these methods and associated technologies reach maturity, engineers will be able to make much more informed design choices much more rapidly, through extensive yet efficient design space exploration. Such dramatic qualitative leaps occur rarely, since much of today's technical progress tends to occur in small increments. This is why I am so excited about the work presented in this volume; I fully expect that it will serve as a core reference source both for researchers and practitioners for many years to come.

In closing, I take this opportunity to pay homage to an exceptional individual, an inspirational leader, a dear friend, and a true gentleman, Dr. Robert France. Sadly, Robert passed away earlier this year, but not until he contributed in fundamental ways to the organization of the Dagstuhl workshop whose results are presented in this volume. However, Robert's contribution to the budding field of model-based software engineering goes far beyond that. He was without doubt one of its true pioneers and will always be fondly remembered as such. One of the initiators of the MoDELS conference series – which has become the premier technical venue for publishing and discussing both research and practical work in the domain—Robert was also the founding editor of the *Journal of Software and Systems Modeling* (SoSym) the mainline scientific publication for model-based papers. A patient but persistent man with high technical standards, Robert always strived for cooperation and synergy, drawing all of us working on models and modeling into a diverse and yet unified force, giving thus greater weight to our work and our messages. He worked tirelessly, not hesitating in his efforts even after he was diagnosed with a fatal disease. Thus let this volume be a tribute to this lovely and important human being, to whom we all owe much.

September 2015   Bran Selić

Preface

This book is a result of the 2014 Dagstuhl seminar no. 14412 entitled "Globalizing Domain-Specific Languages."[1] This Dagstuhl seminar provided a forum in which discussion was focused on the problem of developing complex software systems that span multiple domains of expertise. In the software and system modeling community, research on domain-specific languages (DSLs) aims at providing technologies for developing languages and tools allowing domain experts to efficiently develop system solutions in a particular domain. Unfortunately, the lack of support for explicitly relating concepts expressed in different DSLs made it difficult for developers to reason about information spread across models describing different system aspects. Supporting coordinated use of DSLs leads to what we call the *globalization of domain-specific languages*.

The goal of the seminar was to develop a research initiative that broadens the DSL research focus beyond the development of independent DSLs to one that supports globalized DSLs, that is, DSLs that facilitate coordination of work across different domains of expertise. In the globalized DSLs vision, integrated DSLs provide the means for teams working on systems that span many specialized domains and concerns to determine how their work on a particular aspect influences work on other aspects.

September 2015

Betty H.C. Cheng
Benoit Combemale
Robert B. France
Jean-Marc Jézéquel
Bernhard Rumpe

---

[1] http://www.dagstuhl.de/14412

Organization

Organizers

Betty H.C. Cheng   Michigan State University - East Lansing, USA
Benoit Combemale   University of Rennes and Inria, France
Robert B. France   Colorado State University, USA
Jean-Marc Jezequel   University of Rennes, France
Bernhard Rumpe   RWTH Aachen, Germany

Participants

Colin Atkinson
Cedric Brun
Barrett Bryant
Benoit Caillaud
Betty H.C. Cheng
Tony Clark
Siobhn Clarke
Benoit Combemale
Julien Deantoni
Thomas Degueule
Robert B. France
Ulrich Frank
Jean-Marc Jezequel
Gabor Karsai

Ralf Lämmel
Marjan Mernik
Pieter J. Mosterman
Oscar Nierstrasz
Bernhard Rumpe
Martin Schindler
Friedrich Steimann
Eugene Syriani
Janos Sztipanovits
Juha-Pekka Tolvanen
Antonio Vallecillo
Mark van den Brand
Markus Völter

Sponsoring Initiatives

The GEMOC Initiative, see http://gemoc.org
The ReMoDD Initiative, see http://www.cs.colostate.edu/remodd

Tribute to Robert B. France

At the time of finalizing this book, we were devastated to learn of the passing of Prof. Robert B. France, on the evening of Sunday, February 15, 2015. His passing was painless, after a battle against cancer. He was 54 years old. Robert B. France was one of the initiators of the Dagstuhl seminar no. 14412, fully devoted in the organization, even during the seminar itself, while already suffering from his illness. We dedicate this book to his memory.

Robert's Scientific Life

Robert started his scientific life at the University of the West Indies, St. Augustine, Trinidad and Tobago in the Caribbean. He graduated in 1984 and began working as a computer specialist in a project called USAID Census in the St. Vincent office of a US company. In 1986, he moved on to the Massey University in Palmerston, New Zealand, where he received his PhD in Computer Science in 1990. From 1990 to 1992, he worked as a postdoctoral fellow at the University of Maryland, Institute for Advanced Computer Studies, USA.

Robert was appointed as an assistant professor at the Computer Science and Engineering Department, Florida Atlantic University in Boca Raton, Florida, and stayed there for six years (1992–1998). In 1999, he moved to the Colorado State University (CSU) in Fort Collins as tenured Associate Professor and was promoted to Full Professor in 2004.

In the period 2006–2007, Robert spent his sabbatical year at Lancaster University in the UK and at IRISA/Inria in Rennes, France. He also made a number of extended scientific visits: to the University of Nice in 2009 and 2012, to SINTEF, Norway, in 2009 and 2011, and the University of Pau in 2003. From 2011, he held a position as visiting Adjunct Professor at the University of the West Indies. In his visits and travels, he was often accompanied by his wife, Sheriffa.

Robert was active at CSU in both organizational and scientific positions for as long as his health allowed him and even helped to organize the Modularity Conference, which took place in Fort Collins in March 2015.

During his scientific life, Robert made a remarkable number of research contributions. His CV (last updated in August 2014) lists:

- 33 journal articles
- 10 book chapters
- One invited paper
- 107 refereed conference papers
- 40 refereed workshop papers
- 13 proceedings and journal editorials

And we know that more papers with his name are still being published. As of March 20, 2015, DBLP lists 236 published entries co-authored by Robert, including informal summaries and SoSyM editorials, and an astonishing list of 223 collaborating authors. Google Scholar lists 387 entries! Since he was an Editor-in-Chief of SoSyM from its inception, Robert was never allowed to publish his work there. Therefore his modeling papers were mostly published at conferences. Otherwise, we are sure that his journal paper count would have been even higher!

In addition to his amazing research productivity and a 16-year labor-intensive commitment to SoSyM, Robert was also an active member of IEEE-CS, ACM, and the OMG. In addition, he served on one of the UML task forces as part of his OMG participation. Robert served as a keynote speaker, invited panelist, panel moderator, invited speaker, summer school lecturer, and, in addition, gave numerous talks at companies and conferences all around the world. He also served as an Associate Editor of *IEEE Computer* (2006–2012) and the *Journal of Software Testing, Verification and Reliability* (2006–2015). Furthermore, he cared deeply about the computer science educational curriculum, serving on the IEEE Computer Society Educational Activities Board (2011–2013). However, his most sustainable scientific service achievement was the role he played in establishing the UML/MODELS conference series. He was the general chair and the local arrangements chair of the first UML/MODELS conference held in Fort Collins in 1999, right after an initial UML workshop in France in 1998. This conference series brought together a research community that eventually made SoSyM the success it is today.

Robert Was an Outstanding Researcher

He was a pioneer in the cross-fertilization of formal methods and informal or semi-formal specification languages used in software engineering. His work provided the scientific foundations of the "integrated methods" which have evolved into a rigorous model-driven engineering (MDE). His contributions in the fields of languages, verification, and modeling have provided the mathematical tools used in the design of critical systems. The exceptional quality of his work on modeling, and his contribution to the object-oriented programming and modeling community, was honored in 2014 with the AITO Dahl-Nygaard Senior Prize, awarded on the occasion of the ECOOP conference. The steering committee of the MODELS conference also awarded him in January 2015 the first MODELS Career award.

Robert Was a Recognized Teacher

Robert was recognized for his teaching skills, his proximity with the students, and his ability to share his vision. Sharing knowledge with students always concerned him. He actively participated in the democratization of computer science education, being a member of the Steering Committee of the "IEEE/ACM Computer Science Curriculum Recommendation, CS2013" and head of the committee "IEEE Curricula." He was responsible for the international program REUSSI, and was a mentor for many researchers around the world and helped them to develop a culture and scientific rigor, as well as appreciating the richness of this job. Since 2014, he was Professor Laureate at Colorado State University (CSU), the highest honor that can be awarded to a teacher, recognizing his qualities.

Robert Was Passionate About the Animation of the Scientific Community

Robert was a founding member of the pUML initiative to define a formal semantics for the UML standard. He organized the first UML conference in 1999 in Denver, and the first edition of the newly renamed MODELS conference in 2005 at Montego Bay, Jamaica. He was also a founding member and editor-in-chief of the *SoSyM Journal*. More recently, he promoted various initiatives to take a new step in MDE through a maturation phase: the ReMoDD initiative, which aims at the creation of a repository of models to build experimental results that are sound and reproducible; and the GEMOC initiative, which aims to develop the foundations, methods, and tools to facilitate the creation, integration, and automated processing of heterogeneous modeling languages.

Robert Was a Child of the Caribbean

Always concerned with providing excellent training, he worked a lot to enable young researchers to access studies, build their academic networks, and benefit from exceptional collaborations. He devoted his energy to allow Caribbean students to access their expected studies. These efforts have become part of the heritage of the Caribbean, awarded in 2014 by the Institute of Caribbean Studies.

Contents

On the Globalization of Domain-Specific Languages

Betty H.C. Cheng[1], Benoit Combemale[2,3]([✉]), Robert B. France[4],
Jean-Marc Jézéquel[2], and Bernhard Rumpe[5]

[1] Michigan State University, East Lansing, USA
[2] University of Rennes, Rennes, France
[3] Inria, Rennes, France
benoit.combemale@irisa.fr
http://people.irisa.fr/Benoit.Combemale
[4] Colorado State University, Fort Collins, USA
[5] Software Engineering, RWTH Aachen, Aachen, Germany
rumpe@se-rwth.de

Abstract. In the software engineering community, research on domain-specific languages (DSLs) is focused on providing technologies for designing languages and tools that enable domain experts to develop system solutions efficiently. Unfortunately, the current lack of support to explicitly relate concepts expressed in different DSLs makes it difficult for software and system engineers to reason about information distributed across models or programs describing different system aspects, at different levels of abstraction. Supporting the coordinated use of DSLs is what we call the *globalization of DSLs*. In this chapter, we introduce a grand challenge of the globalization of DSLs, and we present a few motivating scenarios for such a grand challenge.

Keywords: Domain-specific language · DSL · Globalization of DSLs · Model coordination · Modelling

1 Introduction

The development of current and future complex software-based systems such as avionic, intelligent transportation, smart grid, and smart city and building lifecycle management systems, requires experts from diverse domains to work in a coordinated manner on different aspects of the system. For example, the development of a software system that provides energy-efficient building lifecycle management support for energy-aware development, occupation, maintenance, and demolition of smart buildings, typically requires a system development team that includes experts from a variety of domains, including building architecture, material sciences, environmental sciences, energy management, urban/city/town planning, cybersecurity, software engineering, and sensor networks. Each domain has its own knowledge space that is supported by specialized software languages, techniques, and tools. A major problem facing such development teams is how

B.H.C. Cheng et al. (Eds.): Globalizing Domain-Specific Languages, LNCS 9400, pp. 1–6, 2015.
DOI: 10.1007/978-3-319-26172-0_1

to bridge the expertise gap between the diverse domains during system development. Communication among the different domain experts is difficult to achieve due to the lack of a common vocabulary and/or mechanisms that effectively relate domain-specific system information expressed in the different models, tools, techniques, and processes used by the domain experts. Coordination of development activities across the different domains of expertise is particularly necessary when the domains are intertwined, that is, when system decisions made by experts in one domain depends on or influences decisions made by experts in other domains. This type of dependency is common in modern complex systems and can add significant complexity to these systems.

2   Domain-Specific (Modeling) Languages

Model-Driven Engineering (MDE) aims at reducing the accidental complexity associated with developing complex software-intensive systems [8]. A primary source of accidental complexity is the large gap between the high-level concepts used by domain experts to express their problem statements and the low-level abstractions provided by general-purpose programming languages [4]. Manually bridging this gap, particularly in the presence of changing requirements, is costly in terms of both time and effort. MDE approaches address this problem through the use of modeling techniques that support separation of concerns and automated generation of major system artifacts (*e.g.*, test cases, implementations) from models. In MDE, a model describes an aspect of a system and is typically created for specific development purposes. Separation of concerns is supported through the use of different modeling languages, each providing constructs based on abstractions that are specific to an aspect of a system. For example, Generalized Stochastic Petri Nets can be used to create performance models [1], while the notation provided by the Simulink[1] tool is adapted to simulation models. MDE technologies also provide support for manipulating models; for example, there exists tool support for querying, transforming, merging, and analyzing (including executing) models. As such, modeling languages are at the core of MDE.

Incorporating domain-specific concepts and best practices development experience into MDE technologies can significantly improve developer productivity and system quality. This realization has led to work, starting in the late nineties, on MDE-based language workbenches that support the development of domain-specific (modeling) languages (DSLs) and associated tools (e.g., model editors and code generators) [3]. A DSL provides a bridge between the (problem) space in which domain experts work and the implementation (programming) space. Domains in which DSLs have been developed and used include those for automotive, avionics, and cyber-physical systems (CPS). More and more details are also used to describe technical domains, such as configuration of distributed systems and communication networks, deployment structures, mappings of high-level messages to low-level signals, or script languages that guide and control the generation, compilation and deployment processes. It is worthwhile to distinguish

---

[1] http://www.mathworks.com/products/simulink.

technological DSLs and application DSLs, and to recognize that typically several of those DSLs need to be coordinated within a given project.

Through an empirical study, Whittle *et al.* identified practices and trends that seem to indicate that DSLs can pave the way for wider industrial adoption of MDE [9]. Research on systematic development of DSLs has produced a technology base that is sufficiently robust to support the integration of DSL development processes into large-scale industrial system development environments. Current DSL workbenches support the development of DSLs to create models that play pivotal roles in different development phases.

Workbenches such as Microsoft's DSL tools[2], MetaCase's MetaEdit+[3], JetBrains's MPS[4], Eclipse Modeling Framework (EMF)[5], MontiCore[6] and the Generic Modeling Environment (GME)[7] support the specification of the abstract syntax, concrete syntax and the static and dynamic semantics of a DSL. These workbenches address the needs of DSL developers in a variety of application domains.

3 A Grand Challenge of the Globalization of DSLs: Looking Ahead

The development of modern complex software-intensive systems often involves the use of multiple DSLs that capture different system aspects [2]. In addition, models of the system aspects are seldom manipulated independently of each other. System engineers are thus faced with the difficult task of relating information presented in different models. For example, a system engineer may need to analyze a system property that requires information scattered in models expressed in different DSLs. Current DSL development workbenches provide good support for developing independent DSLs, but provide little or no support for integrated use of multiple DSLs. The lack of support for explicitly relating concepts expressed in different DSLs makes it difficult for developers to reason about information distributed across different models.

Past research on DSLs focused on their use to bridge the wide problem to implementation gap. A new generation of complex software-intensive systems, for example, smart health, smart grid, smart home, intelligent automation, building energy management, and intelligent transportation systems, presents new opportunities for leveraging modeling languages. The development of these systems requires expertise in a variety of domains. Consequently, different types of stakeholders (e.g., scientists, engineers and end-users) must work in a coordinated manner on various aspects of the system across multiple development phases. DSLs can be used to support the work of domain experts who focus

---

[2] http://www.microsoft.com/en-us/download/details.aspx?id=2379.

[3] http://www.metacase.com/fr/mwb/.

[4] https://www.jetbrains.com/mps.

[5] http://www.eclipse.org/modeling/emf.

[6] http://www.monticore.de.

[7] http://www.isis.vanderbilt.edu/projects/gme/.

on a specific system aspect (e.g., network communication or security), but they can also provide the means for coordinating work across teams specializing in different aspects and across development phases.

Supporting coordinated use of DSLs leads to what we call the *globalization of DSLs*, that is, the use of multiple DSLs to support coordinated development of diverse aspects of a system. We can make an analogy with globalization in the real world, in which relationships are established between sovereign countries to regulate interactions (e.g., travel and commerce related interactions), while preserving each country's independent existence. The term "DSL globalization" is used to highlight the overarching objective that DSLs developed in an independent manner to meet the specific needs of domain experts should also have an associated framework that regulates interactions needed to support collaboration and work coordination across different system domains.

Globalized DSLs are intended to support the following critical aspects of developing complex systems: communication across teams working on different aspects, coordination of work across the teams, and well-defined management of the teams to ensure product quality. In the vision for globalized DSLs, integrated DSLs support teams working on systems that span many domains and concerns to determine how their work on a particular aspect influences work on other concerns. The objective is to offer support for communicating relevant information, and for coordinating development activities and associated technologies within and across teams. In addition, globalized DSLs should provide support for imposing control over development artifacts produced by multiple teams.

Coordination and related separation of concerns issues have been the focus of software engineering since early work on modularizing software [7]. For example, Parnas' use of the term "work product" to denote a module that can be the source of independent development is also a focus of team demarcation across design and implementation tasks. Modularity in modern software-intensive systems development leads to well-known coordination problems, such as problems associated with coordinating work over temporal, geographic or socio-cultural distances [6]. This line of work has also led to the recognition of socio-technical coordination, including coordination of the stakeholders and the technologies they use to perform their development work, as a major system development challenge [5].

In this context, DSLs can be used to support socio-technical coordination by providing the means for stakeholders to bridge the gap between how they perceive a problem and its solution, and the programming technologies used to implement a solution. DSLs also support coordination of work across multiple teams when they are supported by mechanisms for specifying and managing their interactions. In particular, proper support for coordinated use of DSLs leads to language-based support for social translucence, where the relationships between DSLs are used to extract the information needed to make teams working on different aspects of the system aware of the project activities from other teams.

Such awareness is needed to minimize the counter-productive form of social isolation that can occur when work is distributed across different teams.

4   Motivating Scenarios for the Globalization of DSLs

We now discuss several motivating scenarios for the globalization of DSLs. For each, we describe the typical scenarios encountered by engineers that lead to the need for globalization and show the impact on the overall globalized ecosystem.

Global System Checking: The need for the globalization of DSLs first arises when a system engineer wants to assess a system property that requires crosscutting information scattered in various models. In such a case, system engineers face the difficult task to either build a global structural or behavioral specification of the system from the various models to be able to check the global property or to enhance coordination techniques at hand that enable coordinated models to be checked for global properties.

Model Consistency Checking: In complex software intensive systems where different intertwined DSLs are used to describe the models of the various aspects of the same system, evolving a DSL or a model may have important consequences on the system design as a whole. Since the models of the different system aspects are seldom manipulated in isolation, the development of a model expressed in one DSL can directly influence the form of models created using other DSLs. Similarly, if the different DSLs used for different aspects of a system are tightly coupled, then it is likely that evolving one of them will impact the others. In both cases, syntactic and semantic consistency relationships defined across the DSLs can be used to ensure that the different models and DSLs are consistent with one another.

Traceability for Impact Analysis: As a particular case of consistency checking, one may analyze the impact of a change in one model with respect to other models. For instance, when a requirement changes, one may evaluate the impact on the entire system design. In such cases, traceability links between the various models built all along the development process are required.

Language Evolution: By definition, DSLs evolve as the concepts in a domain and the expert understanding of the domain evolves. As such, it is essential to address consistency between models and DSLs when the DSL specifications change. As a DSL evolves, the conforming models need to evolve accordingly in order to remain consistent with new constructs, new constraints, or changes in the semantics. These consistency demands might lead to a snowball effect, where all the tools, transformations, or workbenches defined around a language need to be updated. In typical large projects, neither all languages nor all models of these languages are evolved in parallel. Therefore, it is necessary to coordinate the parallel use of models in different variants of the same language as well.

Model Composition: Separation of concerns is achieved in MDE by defining as many models as concerns of the system. Eventually, all the different models must be composed in order to support, for example, the generation of the entire system implementation. When different DSLs are used to define the various models, composition rules must be defined between the DSLs.

Simulation: Unfortunately, a simulation of a substantial part of the real world needs to describe different parts and aspects of the world typically using several languages. To run simulations, we need a stable coordination of languages and their respective models for execution. This coordination enables us to understand, for example, whether the models fit together and whether they correctly describe the real world and system to be designed. Examples for coordinated model simulation can be found in various domains, including climate that models whether flow of water, cultivation of areas, run in parallel, and etc. Other simulations are used to understand how control devices in a car cooperate or how the multitude of existing devices in an airplane can be managed by pilots for example.

References

1. Balbo, G.: Introduction to generalized stochastic petri nets. In: Bernardo, M., Hillston, J. (eds.) SFM 2007. LNCS, vol. 4486, pp. 83–131. Springer, Heidelberg (2007)
2. Combemale, B., Deantoni, J., Baudry, B., France, R., Jézéquel, J.-M., Gray, J.: Globalizing modeling languages. Computer **47**, 68–71 (2014)
3. Erdweg, S., et al.: The state of the art in language workbenches. In: Erwig, M., Paige, R.F., Van Wyk, E. (eds.) SLE 2013. LNCS, vol. 8225, pp. 197–217. Springer, Heidelberg (2013)
4. France, R., Rumpe, B.: Model-driven development of complex software: a research roadmap. In: Briand, L.C., Wolf, A.L. (eds.) Proceedings of the Future of Software Engineering Symposium (FOSE 2007), pp. 37–54. IEEE, July 2007
5. Herbsleb, J.D.: Global software engineering: the future of socio-technical coordination. In: Briand, L.C., Wolf, A.L. (eds.) Proceedings of the Future of Software Engineering Symposium (FOSE 2007), pp. 188–198. IEEE, July 2007
6. Herbsleb, J.D., Grinter, R.E.: Architectures, coordination, and distance: Conway's law and beyond. IEEE Softw. **16**, 63–70 (1999)
7. Parnas, D.L.: On the criteria to be used in decomposing systems into modules. Commun. ACM **15**(12), 1053–1058 (1972)
8. Schmidt, D.C.: Guest editor's introduction: model-driven engineering. IEEE Comput. **39**(2), 25–31 (2006)
9. Whittle, J., Hutchinson, J., Rouncefield, M.: The state of practice in model-driven engineering. IEEE Softw. **31**(3), 79–85 (2014)

Conceptual Model of the Globalization for Domain-Specific Languages

Tony Clark[1], Mark van den Brand[2], Benoit Combemale[3]([⊠]),
and Bernhard Rumpe[4]

[1] Middlesex University, London, UK
[2] TU Eindhoven, Eindhoven, Netherlands
[3] University of Rennes and Inria, Rennes, France
benoit.combemale@irisa.fr
[4] Software Engineering, RWTH Aachen, Aachen, Germany

Abstract. Domain Specific Languages (DSL) have received some prominence recently. Designing a DSL and all their tools is still cumbersome and lots of work. Engineering of DSLs is still at infancy, not even the terms have been coined and agreed on. In particular *globalization* and all its consequences need to be precisely defined and discussed. This chapter provides a definition of the relevant terms and relates them, such that a conceptual model emerges. The authors think that this clarification of terms and the meaning will foster the field of efficient DSL definition and evolution in the future.

Keywords: Globalized DSLs · Conceptual model

1 Towards a Conceptual Model of Globalization

Software Engineering, unlike other engineering disciplines, such as *Civil*, *Chemical* or *Material*, deals with constructing precise descriptions of highly complex systems, where each new application contains structure and behaviour that is essentially unique. In essence, each new application is a novel theory of structure and execution, and requires a way of expressing this meta-information [2]. Traditionally *General Purpose Languages* (GPLs) have been used to encode the theories in executable, but implicit forms (e.g., libraries). However recent advances in language engineering technologies have made it possible to develop *Domain Specific Languages* (DSLs) each of which is more suited to encoding theories relating to specific application domains [4].

Modern applications tend to be large, heterogeneous and distributed, involving the use of many different languages including mixtures of GPLs and DSLs. Given that an application consists of many different sub-systems written in different languages, there is a requirement to ensure that the languages and therefore the sub-systems work together effectively and must share the same concepts (theories). Sub-systems written in DSLs are attractive because the languages can provide better support for the specific application domains, however they

© Springer International Publishing Switzerland 2015
B.H.C. Cheng et al. (Eds.): Globalizing Domain-Specific Languages, LNCS 9400, pp. 7–20, 2015.
DOI: 10.1007/978-3-319-26172-0_2

tend to be less mature than their GPL counterparts and therefore there is an interesting research challenge: how to achieve language globalization [1] whereby GPLs and DSLs can co-exist and work together in order to achieve a high quality assured system.

DSLs introduce *meta-architectures* into the process of systems development. Naur [2] argues that systems development is the process of encoding theories about a specific system into GPLs. By the same argument, DSLs involve the process of encoding theories of a complete domain. Encoding a system theory into a GPL involves finding a way of mapping the theorems into the (often computationally-centric) domain supported by the GPL, even if this is done via libraries; whereas encoding a system theory into a DSL requires less cognitive dissonance. At least at the conceptual level, integration respectively globalization is achieved by finding mappings between the different theories that make up a system such that the mappings are maintained when mapped to the implementation languages.

A system that requires no integration with respect to globalization effort must be implemented in a single perfect DSL. Increased use of separate DSLs within a system will require mappings between the distinct theories, but will require no *implementation* mappings to be applied to the point-wise correspondences. This is possible if the DSLs are implemented using the same programming language or framework. A hybrid DSL/GPL system will need to deal with several such implementation mappings where the domain-specific nature of the theories has been lost through an implementation encoding; finally a GPL-only system must face a situation where all mappings are computationally encoded.

There has been very little exploration of the foundations and concepts that underpin methods and technologies needed to address the challenges of globalization such as those outlined above. The aim of this chapter is to perform a domain analysis for globalization such as defined in Definition 7 and to propose a conceptual model that can be used to organise and classify these challenges. In attempting to produce such a model we will encounter issues for which there are no current or no generally accepted solutions; these will be listed as research challenges at the end of the chapter.

2   Basic Terms

Definition 1 (Model). *A model has three characteristics: There is an original that it models. The model is an abstraction with respect to the original. The model has a purpose with respect to the original. (Definition to Stachowiak, 1973) [3].*

Models are used in almost every science and engineering discipline for quite some time and for a variety of purposes. Some are prescriptive, where the model is developed before the system and used to describe and / or predict the systems properties. In natural and social sciences models are used to describe the systems under study (from subatomic particles to galaxies, from molecules to cells to animal behavior to societal behavior) and thus to understand (part) of these systems. It is important to precisely define the purpose of the model, in order to understand its appropriateness of the model as abstraction from the original. The intended purposes are often clarified by the questions that a model should be able to answer.

Modelling is a rather old mechanism, computer science, however has made it possible that models are also shared between humans and computers, which led to the necessity to make modeling more explicit and more precise. Modelling languages necessarily emerged.

Definition 2 (Language). *A language is a means for communication between humans, machines, and humans and machines. A language describes the set of possible sentences that may be communicated between the stakeholders.*

Languages allow us to describe various things, among others expressing data (structure), computations (behavior), interaction, requirements, physical structure, networking structure, etc. As a consequence languages are amenable to both mechanical and cognitive processing. Usually sentences are handled as individually storable, versionable and manipulable artifacts. So it is legal to identify the sentence with the artifact that contains the sentence.

While the definition does not explicitly speak about language semantics or potential forms of use, a language normally also intends a semantics for its sentences as well as a pragmatics to clarify the forms of use.

Definition 3 (Domain Specific Language (DSL)). *A DSL is a language that is specifically dedicated to a domain of interest.*

DSLs are therefore typically restricted, both in the domain, where they are used and in their expressiveness. This on the other hand gives us the advantage to more easily design the language including syntax and semantics of all the language elements. A DSL should be seen in contrast to a general-purpose language (GPL) that is broadly applicable without any feature for a particular domain. In particular programming languages are typically GPL, but the Unified Modeling Language also is a general-purpose and thus domain agnostic language. If a DSL is used for modeling purposes, then we speak of a domain specific modeling language or DSML.

While a language set of sentences is usually infinite, we need a finite, comprehensive form to define a language. We distinguish the terms language and language definition, to make it precise what we are speaking about. There are many definitions for the same language and in the globalization context we manipulate language definitions, while defining new languages. For example the Java languages is a set of sentences (called programs) and can be described by a variety of mechanisms, including different forms of grammars.

Definition 4 (Language Definition). *A language is defined by the following concepts:*

- *Concrete syntax: e.g. in textual, tabular, or graphical form describing the set of sentences of the language.*
- *Abstract syntax: describing essential concepts and structure of the sentences without semantically irrelevant concrete sugar.*
- *Static semantics (or context conditions): Is a boolean predicate based on the concrete respectively abstract syntax. Sentences that fulfill the static semantics are called well-formed. They obey the context (scope, type system, etc.)*
- *Meaning (or dynamic semantics) of the sentences e.g. as operational, denotational, or axiomatic semantics.*

3   DSL Integration

A language that is used as the basis of mechanical processing consists of a collection of components including syntax, well-formedness checking, and semantics. Following Naur, we abstract from the implementation of a language to its definition, in which case the language consists of a collection of integrated theories. Each theory consists of theorems that relate to one particular aspect of the language, for example concrete syntax (its grammar), type checking, security, execution, memory usage, *etc.* In addition, a collection of mappings between the theories ensures that they work collectively to answer any question that is of interest relating to the language, for example linking information contained in a syntax-theorem to elements used in a type-theorem and a corresponding operational theorem.

The computational models used by GPLs have been under development for many years and are rather mature, though not really standardized. A number of meta-languages for expressing language-based theories have grown up around these models, for example λ-calculi, Hoare Logic, natural deduction systems, variants of states transition systems, petri-nets and pi-calculi. Deduction within these systems is well understood and general purpose, and it is possible to map from one to another.

Our conceptualisation should not be limited to those aspects of systems that are known to be supported by practical tools (parsers, type-checkers, compilers, and run-time systems). We wish to think of *any* aspect of a system being expressed using a theory that co-exists with all other aspectual theories so that an entire system including its history and its future is captured by a family of co-dependent theories. Therefore, theories relating to design co-exist with theories relating to security or privacy, and theories relating to distributed development can be related to theories about usability or hardware failure rates.

If a system is defined using these meta-languages then there is a good correspondence between GPLs and the resulting theories. However, following Naur, a system consists of a collection of domain-specific theories. For example a financial system may contain a theory about Sarbanes-Oxley or a pan-european education system may contain a theory about the Bologna Process. The domain-specific theories are not necessarily computational, but must be encoded within computational theories in order to achieve a practical system.

Encoding domain-specific theories within GPL computational theories, via libraries, leads to a problem that DSLs address. As an extreme example, consider a simple information system LibSys consisting of theories relating to library borrowing. The LibSys theories are not computational in the sense that they describe a step-by-step process, they simply define the arrangements of information that must hold and the services that are offered. In contrast, consider a machine that processes binary information in terms of a stack, a heap and a simple instruction set. There is a theory M that describes computations that are performed given specific starting states for the machine. Our challenge is to encode the LibSys theory into the M theory.

To understand and describe a language it is useful to regard it as a collection of inter-related theories which themselves are denoted in a collection of meta-languages, each of which is itself a language. This regress is usually grounded by using meta-languages that are well-understood and that do not require further elaboration. Introducing DSLs however means that there is an extra level of language definition that requires meta-languages to be defined on a per-application basis. This leads us to meta-meta-languages being the basis for definition, but also provides scope for the basic meta-meta-language to be fixed for all DSLs that are used in an application. Whilst this is not always possible, it is attractive because it facilitates the relationships between theories that are required for globalization.

4   Language Components and Interfaces

The integration of languages works best, when we use modularization techniques similar to those available for programming. We therefore propose the use of language components.

A language component captures all information about the language and exposes aspects to language users. Globalization is achieved by mapping between aspects in terms of the concrete interface data. The idea of language definition liberates us from having to say how the language is implemented and also how the interfaces are achieved.

Definition 5 (Language Component). *A language component (aka. language module or language unit) is a reusable encapsulation of a, possibly incomplete, language. A language component includes a language definition and might include explicit provided and required language interfaces.*

A language component may be incomplete in three ways: First it may be parameterized, such that other language components can be plugged in. Second the language component may itself be dedicated for composition and thus not be of (much) use as standalone language. That also means that each language itself is a language component, that however is free of parameters and complete in that sense that it can be used purposeful.

Third, a language may be incomplete in its components. While the main ingredient of a language, namely the abstract syntax must always be given, a language component may omit the concrete syntax or a definition of the semantic domain and mapping. For an engineering point of view, it may also omit editor, compiler, generator, and other operational realizations useful for a language. We assume that language adaptations take place to add missing constituents of a language.

Globalization of components enforce interfaces, where components are glued together.

Definition 6 (Language Interface). *A language interface is a relevant abstraction for a specific purpose of a provided or required part of a language component. An interface can be defined manually in a separate artifact or inferred automatically from the language component definition.*

This is a very general description for language interfaces that will have different characteristics dependent on languages that are interfaced and the purpose of the composition. It may be a syntactic interface, connecting syntax, may be an interface describing imported and exported types, variables and other kinds of names, or maybe a purely semantic interface allowing to connect the semantics of language components. Technical interfaces also may connect editors, analyzers, synthesizers or code generators for the respective language components (Fig. 1).

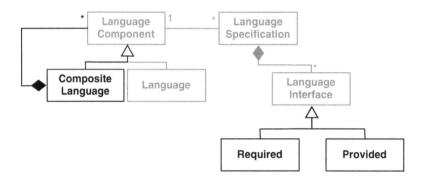

Fig. 1. Language component (open question!)

Figure 2 gives a simple view of globalization in terms of *language definitions*. A language definition captures the information about a language in a technology independent manner, *i.e.*, without recourse to implementation technologies such as parsers, compilers, run-time systems *etc.*

The idea is that a language definition is the essential characterising information about a language. All aspects of a language are captured in principle, however some will be of more use than others with respect to globalization. For example, if globalization is to occur exclusively at run-time then the syntactic definition of a language (the set of program phrases) is of no interest; whereas, if an editor is to be used to integrate two or more languages then syntax may be the only aspect of interest.

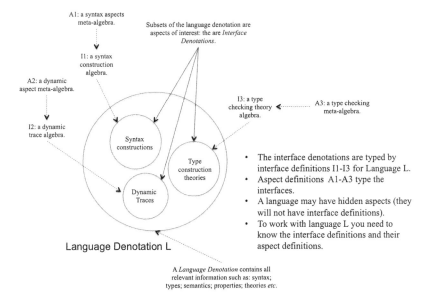

Fig. 2. Language components and interfaces

5   Globalization

Definition 7 (Globalization). *Globalization deals with the purposeful construction, adaptation, coordination and integration of explicitly defined languages, to be amenable to mechanical and cognitive processing, with the goal of improving quality and reducing the cost of system development.*

Globalization is achieved (partially or wholly) in terms of syntactic and/or semantic integration from the perspective of globalization stakeholders. Globalization addresses all aspects of the life-cycles of languages and the systems developed with them and therefore affects their development and coordination of multiple concerns, methods, documentation, tools, variations and maintenance. Language globalization affects several levels, such as type or meta-type, and may be achieved statically or dynamically, or a mixture of both.

It is useful to be aware of the different stakeholders and especially their individual and therefore often conflicting goals and backgrounds (Fig. 3).

Definition 8 (Globalization Stakeholder). *Any person who is affected by the definition or use of a language or its components is a globalization stakeholder.*

Globalization stakeholders include the globalization strategist who is responsible for the globalization strategy for an organisation; the language engineers that develop or prepare languages to be globalized; language integrators that ensure that two or more languages are globalized; software and system engineers that use a collection of globalized languages for manipulating artifacts (Fig. 4).

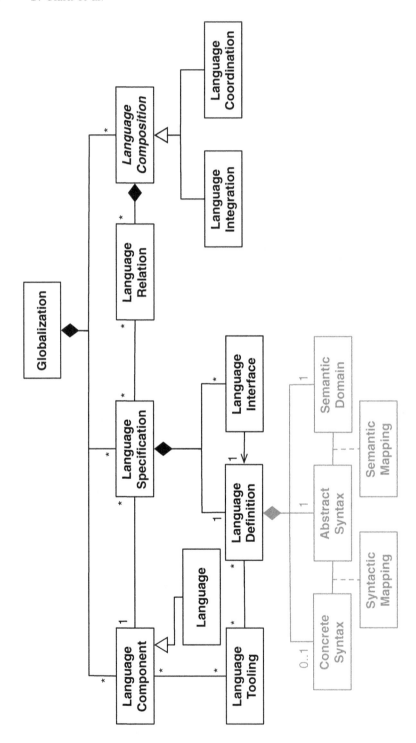

Fig. 3. Conceptual model for the globalization of DSLs

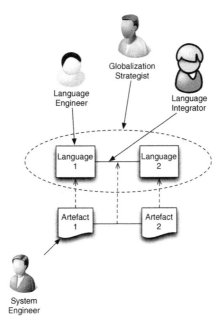

Fig. 4. Globalization stakeholders

Globalization will involve at least two but usually more language definitions. Integration will occur in terms of the information contained in different aspects. The information used for integration is defined by the language interface since they will be used in mappings between languages. For example, if two different languages have type systems then they must expose their respective type definitions to a mapping that associates types from one language to corresponding types in the other.

Globalization is *specified* in terms of language definitions and the specification of relations between them. Once globalization is specified, it must be implemented. Clever implementation techniques must be found that achieve efficient mappings between the required aspects.

6 Language Relations

We examine the various existing forms of relationships between languages:

Definition 9 (Language Relation). *A language relation relates the sentences of multiple languages.*

In simple cases, only two languages respectively their sentences are related. However, it may be that in a relation sets of sentences are related to each other on both sides. This captures e.g. composition and slicing as relations.

If a relation needs to be effectively executed, an algorithmic mapping is necessary to realize the relation:

Definition 10 (Language Mapping). *A language mapping is a language rela-*
tion that has an algorithmic, effectively executable realization that maps sen-
tences of the source languages to sentences of the target languages.

As many languages do have infinitely many sentences, a relation has to be
expressed in a finite form for example using the language definitions. So instead
of relating entire sentences of the languages, usually concepts of the syntax structure or the semantic structure are related. The relation can range from purely
syntax based to a relation between the semantic domains. Several interesting
cases are:

- If some of the syntax constructs and the corresponding semantics of the languages are identical the relation for these constructs is the identity. It is sufficient that the abstract syntax is identical, the concrete syntax may differ.
- If the abstract syntax constructs differ but the semantic domains are identical,
  then there is no need for a semantic integration anymore. For an even tighter
  coupling a syntax based relation can be added, that is consistent with the
  semantics relation.
- If both differ syntactical and semantical relations can be provided.
- The case that the abstract syntax is the same, but the corresponding semantics
  differs should be avoided, because this leads to unsolvable problems. However,
  it may be that the abstract syntax is the same, but the semantics encoding
  differs even though the intended meaning of both languages is the same. In
  this case a relation of between the semantics (respectively their encodings)
  should be provided.

The complexity of the semantic relation depends on the "distance" between
the semantic domains of both languages. While we don't feel able to fully define
the term "distance" here, we might agree that the larger the "distance" between
two languages is, the deeper the "encoding" of one language in the other needs
to be. E.g. state machines can be "deeply" encoded to a relational database
schema, by encoding their entire syntactic structure using a state and transition
table, while a relation between class diagrams and relational data base schemata
can be relatively "shallow". If may even be not feasible to define a semantic
relation. The syntactic relation may be influenced by the fact that information
has to be removed or created.

The type of mappings used in globalization between language definitions
is defined in terms of the types of the constituent interfaces. For example, if
two type-systems are defined using different meta-languages then the mapping
is a relation between the meta-languages. The types of the interfaces are called
aspects of the language. As noted above, some aspects may be of more importance
to globalization than others, and some aspects may be limited to the construction
of the definitions, *i.e.*, hidden to any external language user.

7   Composition

Definition 11 (Language Composition). *This is an abstract concept that achieves globalization in terms of multiple languages working together to achieve a common goal.*

Composition may be achieved using a number of strategies including language integration and language coordination. The composition of two or more languages may require additional information in the form of a correspondence between the syntax and/or semantics of the constituent languages. A language can be decomposed to produce two or more languages in which case the decomposition is to be viewed as the inverse of the corresponding composition.

Our claim is that globalization requirements can be conceptualized in terms of language definitions, their interface definitions and associated aspect definitions. A globalization requirement for a set of language definitions S involves the specification of a new language definition L such that a collection of constraints holds between L and S. The language L is the required globalization language.

Consider two languages L1 and L2 and a requirement to globalize with respect to both syntax and operational semantics. This might be expressed as the construction of a new language definition where the globalization requirement is expressed in terms of the syntax and operational semantics interface definitions (that are required to be present by reference to the associated aspect definitions). Such a requirement might involve the definition of two language transformations p1 and p2 that are defined in terms of the interface definitions and capture the syntax and operational semantics of the language L3 as shown in Fig. 5.

Language components contain the definitions of interfaces that correspond to theories about aspects of the languages that are required for globalization. As such, language components are themselves structured elements that can be subject to transformation and combination with other language components. Therefore, we envisage a calculus of language module construction, combination and transformation operators that characterise globalization.

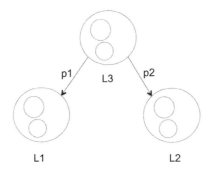

L3 is specified in terms of projections p1 and p2.

Fig. 5. Language composition

8   Language Coordination

The coordination of several languages is a special, loose form of composition.

Definition 12 (Language Coordination). *Language Coordination is a form of composition where individual sentences of the coordinated languages are collaborating to achieve a common goal.*

As a consequence of this definition is that, while the languages are coordinated for a specific purpose, the artifacts (containing the sentences) of the coordinated languages remain as individual artifacts. This allows to independently reuse them, and include artifacts of each of the languages in the coordination.

Coordination implies that the controlled languages remain independent. For example, dynamic coordination might be achieved by registering an observer with two independent run-time systems that propagates changes from one run-time to another. Language coordination is to be contrasted with language integration where two or more languages are merged to produce a new language.

Coordination can be achieved via sharing concepts with the same semantics. The corresponding models do not exchange information explicitly, but reasoning about artifacts related to shared semantic concepts becomes easier. Coordination can also be achieved via sharing of concepts with different semantics. The corresponding models have to exchange information explicitly. Tools that manipulate the models should provide facilities to exchange of information. The information can data or control based.

As an example, consider a globalization requirement for two DSLs. The first DSL L1 manages a data-base and provides a collection of event-based rules. Events occur when data changes. Rule-actions can cause further updates to the data. The second DSL L2 defines simple form-based input screens. Buttons can occur on forms. The language component for L1 provides an event aspect and a data aspect. A hidden aspect of L1 is a sequence of event-driven data-base traces. The language component for L2 provides a button-press aspect and a form-content aspect. A hidden aspect of L2 is a button-press driven sequence of form-traces. The mapping that specifies the globalization of L1 and L2 associates the events from L1 with the button presses of L2 and the data states of L1 with the form-content of L2.

The implementation of the globalization specification may require some form of common data representation to be defined to that the form information is available to the data-base when the event is raised. In addition, a communication mechanism must be implemented that ensures an event is raised in L1 when a button is pressed in L2. There are many such implementation architectures that would be consistent with the globalization specification.

9   Language Integration

Another major form of language composition is the integration of two languages:

Definition 13 (Language Integration). *Language Integration is the production of a new language from a set of individual languages.*

The resulting language has a its own set of sentences, but each sentence has "sub-sentences" which come from the individual sub-languages. For modeling languages we also call those constituencies "model components" in correspondence to the language components.

An integrated language is not required to exhibit all language concepts of its sublanguages. For example, state machines and Java might be integrated to produce a new state machine language that uses Java statements as actions and Java boolean expressions as guards.

Language integration has been studied since it became clear that the definition of new languages is complex and error-prone. Language integration is the type of form of the reuse of individual components and heavily relies on a crisp and well-defined notion of language interface, because this is the place where languages are syntactically integrated and where static semantics as well as dynamic semantics has to conform.

10   Towards the Conceptualisation of the Globalization of DSLs

This article defines a number of terms in an abstract way for dealing with the globalization of DSLs and relates them in various ways. However, in practical use there are pretty many open questions, to answer.

1. What is a language interface?
2. What is a language component?
3. What is language composition?
4. How to use a language interface?
5. How to facilitate language integrations?
6. How to facilitate language coordination?
7. Are there other forms of language composition?
8. What is an appropriate formulation for language relation?
9. How does a language relation relate to a language concept relation?
10. Can we identify general mechanisms for language composition or is composition highly specific to syntax, semantics and purpose of languages?

The key to globalization is the ability for all stakeholders to understand how the interaction between models can be facilitated via the relationships between the constituent languages. It would appear that a fruitful way to achieve this is to apply a component based approach to language composition. Such an approach implies a clear definition of language component and language interface, however this is an open research question at this stage. Therefore, an important area for future research should be to conceptualise language components and to propose concrete mechanisms for component and interface definitions. For example, should interfaces be models? How can existing languages be wrapped to produce components? How can components be linked together via interfaces? What should a provided and required interface for a language be? If interfaces are models are there such things as meta-interfaces? Can interfaces provide access to all levels of language (instance, model, meta-model)?

System developers within a globalization context should be, as far as possible, unaware of the integration machinery when developing their models. This is a significant research challenge for tool developers. In addition to tooling, a new methodology for MDE may be required in order to guide globalization stakeholders.

In addition to the primary concepts defined in this chapter, the following issues are potentially relevant to successfully achieving globalization: language libraries; language viewpoints; sub-languages; language transformation and adaptation; language construction; language and system quality. We do not have definitions for these terms in the context of globalization and therefore they should be considered as areas for further work.

References

1. Combemale, B., Deantoni, J., Baudry, B., France, R., Jézéquel, J.-M., Gray, J.: Globalizing Modeling Languages. IEEE Comput. **47**(6), 68–71 (2014)
2. Naur, P.: Programming as theory building. Microprocess. Microprogram. **15**(5), 253–261 (1985)
3. Stachowiak, H.: Allgemeine Modelltheorie. Springer-Verlag, Wien, New York (1973)
4. Van Deursen, A., Klint, P., Visser, J.: Domain-specific languages: an annotated bibliography. ACM Sigplan Not. **35**(6), 36 (2000). http://homepages.cwi.nl/paulk/publications/Sigplan00.ps

Motivating Use Cases
for the Globalization of DSLs

Betty H.C. Cheng[1]($\boxtimes$), Thomas Degueule[2], Colin Atkinson[3], Siobhan Clarke[4],
Ulrich Frank[5], Pieter J. Mosterman[6,7], and Janos Sztipanovits[8]

[1] Michigan State University, East Lansing, USA
`chengb@cse.msu.edu`
[2] University of Rennes and Inria, Rennes, France
[3] University of Mannheim, Mannheim, Germany
[4] Trinity College, Dublin, Republic of Ireland
[5] University of Duisburg-Essen, Essen, Germany
[6] MathWorks, Natick, USA
[7] McGill University, Montreal, Canada
[8] Vanderbilt University, Nashville, USA

Abstract. The development of complex software-intensive systems
involves many stakeholders who contribute their expertise on specific
aspects of the system under construction. Domain-specific languages
(DSLs) are typically used by stakeholders to express their knowledge
of the system using dedicated tools and abstractions. In this chapter, we
explore different scenarios that lead to the globalization of DSLs through
two motivating case studies – a command and control wind tunnel and a
smart emergency response system – and outline the concrete engineering
challenges they raise. Finally, we list some of the general research challenges related to the globalization of DSMLs and discuss some promising
approaches for addressing them.

Keywords: Multi-model integration · Language integration

1 Introduction

Languages have been used in the development and evolution of software systems since the beginning of the computer industry. For many years, software
engineers only needed to concern themselves with one language, the one general
purpose programming language typically used to program an application (e.g.
FORTRAN, COBOL, C or Pascal). Today, however, software engineers have to
cope with a vast array of languages, supporting descriptions of different aspects
and parts of software systems from the viewpoints of multiple stakeholders, levels of abstraction and concerns. This creates many new challenges for languages
engineers beyond the traditional need to define a language's syntaxes (concrete
and abstract) and semantics. Now language engineers have to cope with multiple semantic interactions between the entities and concepts described by languages and cope with the co-evolution and management of families of interrelated
languages.

© Springer International Publishing Switzerland 2015
B.H.C. Cheng et al. (Eds.): Globalizing Domain-Specific Languages, LNCS 9400, pp. 21–42, 2015.
DOI: 10.1007/978-3-319-26172-0_3

Traditionally these challenges have been addressed in ad hoc ways, primarily at the level of the entities and concepts described by languages (i.e. at the level of statements made in a language) rather than at the level of the languages themselves (i.e. at the level of language definitions). However, as domain-specific modeling technologies have matured, and the problems of engineering single-purpose language solutions have been mastered, new conceptual tools and technologies for engineering heterogeneous solutions at the language level have started to emerge. Researchers now have the means to create new methodologies and tool ecosystems for combining independently-developed language fragments into new solutions that can leverage the vast amounts of knowledge and experience embedded within language definitions. The challenge of language globalization is to realize this vision.

Language globalization therefore aims to improve the way software systems are developed and evolved with a view to raising software quality and reducing costs. A major source of motivating use cases for this technology can be found in the realm of software systems engineering. Language globalization can be expected to improve the way in which key systems engineering challenges can be addressed, such as enhancing the functionality and information content of software systems, as well as adding new views and view types by which stakeholders can visualize them. This chapter illuminates the key language globalization challenges by exploring the language exploitation opportunities occurring in typical software development use cases. In particular, we present a set of concrete use cases in the context of two real-world example applications. After introducing these two applications and presenting the language engineering challenges they raise, we discuss the resulting research challenges.

2   Command and Control Wind Tunnel (C2WT)

The C2WT[1] is a model-integrated distributed simulation environment developed at the Institute for Software Integrated Systems at Vanderbilt University for complex, multi-modeling simulation tasks frequently required in virtual prototyping, end-to-end mission simulation and resilience studies. The application scenario below led to its original development as a part of an Air Force Office of Scientific Research (AFOSR) project.

2.1   Application: Evaluation of Command and Control Architectures in Mission Scenarios

The evaluation of emerging command and control (C2) architectures necessitates a sophisticated modeling and simulation infrastructure that supports the concurrent modeling, simulation, and evaluation of (1) the C2 system architecture (advanced system-of-systems modeling), (2) the mission environment (scenario

---

[1] https://wiki.isis.vanderbilt.edu/OpenC2WT/.

modeling and generation), and the (3) human organizations and (group and individual) decision-making processes (human performance and man-machine interaction modeling). Using simulated C2 environments to evaluate design concepts, validate new systems and components, and explore hazardous as well as ambiguous scenarios is easily justified from both cost and practicality perspectives.

An example of this application is shown in Fig. 1. The mission scenario focuses on flying teleoperated Unmanned Aerial Vehicles (UAVs) in an urban environment for finding and tracking moving vehicles on the ground [15]. Each UAV is controlled by a human operator who inspects a video stream from the on-board sensor and remotely controls the UAV. The operators coordinate their track and search activities amongst each other and with a remote command center. Mission success is measured in terms of the time required for finding a moving vehicle with specific characteristics and the length of time tracking the vehicle without losing it. The specific evaluation scenarios examine the impact on mission success UAV characteristics (such as mobility, level of autonomy, sensor resolution), network attacks, allocation of decision responsibilities in the C2 architecture, and others.

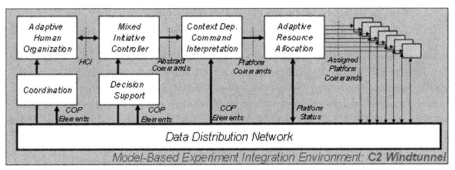

Fig. 1. Command and control (C2) architecture analysis

The scenario identifies a network of interacting simulations (Fig. 2). The individual modeling languages were selected based on the relevance of their respective domains to the simulation goals: Colored Petri Net (CPN) for modeling decision processes and interactions in command and control organizations, Simulink/Stateflow for modeling vehicle dynamics and controller dynamics, DEVS for modeling abstract behavior of software components, OMNeT for

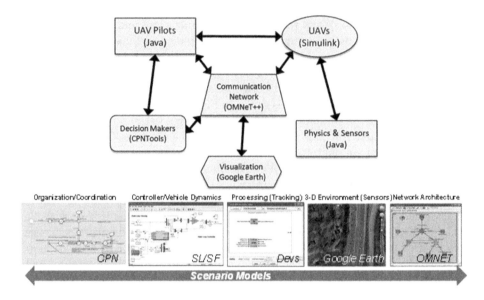

Fig. 2. Modeling languages and technologies involved in the C2WT

modeling communication links, and Google Earth for modeling motion in specific 3D environments. In addition, the overall simulation was executed in real-time interacting with two UAV operators. The choice of modeling languages is strongly motivated by the need for reusing existing model libraries and existing simulators. However, neither of them was designed for incorporating all the other modeling abstractions.

2.2   Technical Challenges

Complex command and control environments have many disparate facets that need to be modeled and simulated. The constituent models include decision processes, dynamics of moving objects in a 3-D environment, sensors and information flows, communication networks, operator work stations, and mission scenarios. The modeling languages have different timing semantics (continuous time, discrete time, discrete event) and data semantics (3-D geometry, commands, physical variables). The simulations running on different simulation engines need to be coordinated, and the data needs to be routed. As a result, a heterogeneous collection of integrated simulations, all acting in a tightly coordinated environment, must be employed.

Individual simulations comprise two parts: a domain-specific model, such as a model of a flight control system in Simulink, and an underlying simulation engine, such as the Simulinks solver. Each modeling language has its own unique execution semantics as implemented by its simulation engine. All of the executions in federated (integrated) simulations must be coordinated in a meaningful way to ensure that the larger C2 simulation environment is useful.

The problems in developing integrated simulations can be decomposed into two integration problems:

Model Integration ensures that the domain models (UAV dynamics model in Simulink, communication channel model in OMNeT, etc.) can be integrated in a semantically consistent manner.

Simulation Integration ensures that execution of simulations can be synchronized by a distributed global clock (that can be kept in synchrony also with the wall clock), the events generated by the individual simulators can be used for event-driven interaction among objects controlled by different simulators, and data can be routed among the simulators under the time constraints required by the progress of the distributed global clock.

Next, we explore these challenges in further detail.

2.3   Model Integration Challenge

There exist several ways to approach the challenge of integrating domain models in a semantically consistent way.

Modeling Language Embedding. Embedding requires an injective structure preserving mapping between one or more DSMLs and a host language. Accordingly, the semantic domain of the host language must be rich enough to provide a common semantic domain for all DSMLs. While from the point of view of time semantics, the continuous time (CT) semantics of Simulink can embed the discrete event (DE) semantics of CPN, DEVS and OMNeT, mapping many of their domain-specific languages constructs onto Simulink constructs would be impractical. Some variant of model embedding is facilitated by the external blocks allowed in some modeling languages (e.g. Modelicas external function calls, and FMU import, Simulinks S-function interface) but they require suppressing many details of an external model, transform it into a simple construct in the host language, therefore they cannot be regarded as an example of model embedding in the usual sense.

Formal Modeling Language Composition. There have been formally established methods for the precise composition of DSMLs in an algebraic/logic framework [15]. The approach introduces a range of composition operators (*includes, restricts, extends, as, pseudo-product* "*", *pseudo-coproduct* "+") with appropriate semantics. These composition operators have been introduced in the FORMULA tool [1] developed by Ethan Jackson at Microsoft Research. While precise and tool-supported, practical full formal treatment in this case study was restricted by the absence of a formal, FORMULA-based specification of the semantics of the constituent modeling languages.

Model Integration Language. In many (if not most) multi-modeling problems, physical or computational objects modeled in different modeling languages need to interact with each other. The interaction might have behavioral, structural, or conceptual meaning. If the semantics of the interaction is restricted only to some shared aspects of the semantics of the individual modeling languages, then the problem can be solved effectively by the specification of a model integration language [24] that includes the specification of a semantic interface for the individual modeling languages and the specification of integration constructs that are not part of either of the integrated modeling languages but support the integration of the models across the semantic interfaces. In the C2WT case study, the purpose of the model integration is the coordination of timed behavior of objects in a 3D space using various forms of communication. The required interaction semantics is discrete event and the data semantics is based on a distributed (but partial) data model that need to be established for the scenario. Consequently, model integration requires the specification of a relatively narrow *semantic interface* for the individual DSMLs and a *Model Integration Language* that is built atop these semantic interfaces, extends them with integration-specific constructs and supports the rapid modeling of arbitrary model integration scenarios.

2.4 A Model Integration Language Solution for C2WT

The technical challenges for the C2WT modeling and simulation application offer a compelling case for using a model integration language. The individual modeling languages are rich and have complex semantics not defined formally (and in addition they evolve independently with new releases). The required interaction semantics across the models is relatively narrow and restricted to only some aspects of the rich semantics of modeling languages. However, these simplifying conditions only mean that the solution is feasible, but not that it is simple.

The primary difficulty in defining a model integration language for the C2WT application is that it requires runtime support for model and simulation integration on a distributed computing platform. Support for model integration means availability of services for data distribution (in real-time scenarios under time constraints), simulation integration means availability of services for distributed time management and interaction control. In fact, the development and use of these services represent the core technical challenges in this application. Fortunately, distributed simulation is important in many application domains, therefore well-developed standard frameworks are available, such as the High Level Architecture (HLA) [4] that was selected as simulation integration platform for C2WT. With this, our task was simplified to developing a C2WT model integration language and related tools. The High-Level Architecture is a standardized architecture for distributed computer simulation systems. Communications between different federates is managed via the Run-Time Infrastructure (RTI) layer – an implementation of the HLA standard.

The HLA standard focuses on three primary areas. The first is time coordination throughout the federation. The evolution of time is a key thread through each of the integrated simulators. Each simulation engine must slave its progression of time to that of the overall HLA clock. The HLA standard provides several methods to accomplish this. Second is coordination of inter-federate messages and shared data objects. The HLA standard provides a publish-and-subscribe mechanism for passing messages and object updates throughout the federation. Third, the HLA standard provides for basic simulation execution control. A limited ability to start, pause, and stop the execution of a simulation is built directly into the HLA standard. The C2WT relies upon the services provided by the RTI during run-time. As HLA is an accepted standard, a number of commercial, academic, and alternate RTI implementations are available. Currently, we use the Portico RTI [2] which provides support for both C++ and Java clients and is compliant with version 1.3 of the HLA standard.

The integrated system is shown in Fig. 3. The simulators are interfaced to the HLA RTI through the simulator federates. The federates use the HLA RTI API for time management, data distribution and execution control. Clearly, the federations capture all of the required code needed to implement the multi-model simulation. We explicitly model this information using the C2WT model integration language, and translate this integration model into federation code. Details, including the metamodels of the integration languages are described in [14]. We used the following strategy to design the C2WT Model Integration Language:

1. The constituent modeling languages remain unchanged,
2. The C2WT model integration language is used for describing the integration (i.e. the system-of-system) architecture,
3. The semantics of the model integration language is provided by the HLA services for time and data management,
4. The semantic interface is the simplest possible required for the integration tasks.

The semantic relationship between federates are defined in the model integration language using two main aspects: the data representation and the data flow. An integration model describes both data representation and data flow elements, and, in some cases, includes special elements as the placeholders for concepts specific to particular simulation engines. Data representation models consist of interaction and object models. Interactions are stateless, and can have parameters, while objects have states, which are represented as a set of attributes. Both interactions and objects are permitted to have inheritance hierarchies. These data representation models directly map to the HLA Federation Object Model (FOM). The federates (interfaces of simulators to HLA) are automatically generated from the integration models. The model integration language was specified by the usual means (informal (MetaGME) and formal (FORMULA) metamodels) and published in [14]. The full open source package is available on the OpenC2WT web site [3].

The set of integrated modeling languages and simulators is open, they do not influence HLA or each other. Currently the integrated modeling languages and engines include Simulink/Stateflow, CPN (Colored Petri Net), NS-2, OMNET, Delta3D, DEVSJava, Google Earth and Java-based custom federates (e.g. operator interface for user interaction in real-time simulation).

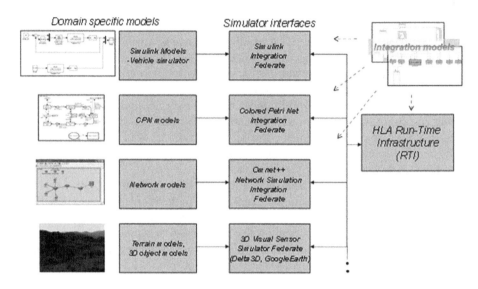

Fig. 3. Integration of DSMLs and Simulators using HLA

3   Smart Emergency Response System (SERS)

A MathWorks Summer Research Internship project [18] developed an automated emergency response system in order to dynamically manage emergency response personnel and equipment to handle emergencies on the roadways in the San Francisco area [20]. The system was then expanded into a Smart Emergency Response System (SERS) [26].

SERS coordinates the dispatch of flight systems (both rotorcraft and fixed-wing aircraft), ground supp:ort vehicles, and search and rescue dogs equipped with a harness to hold electronic devices. A smart device app enables emergency responders and survivors to share information in the field, learn about the current state of response operations, and request assistance. The information from the field as well as aid requests combined with available provisions (e.g., prescription medication, thermal blankets, defibrillators) and the configuration of the vehicle fleet serve as the input to a planning module that computes the time optimal mission. The deployment plan for each of the vehicles is then sent and executed autonomously by the respective vehicles (rotorcraft, fixed wing aircraft, and ground vehicles).

A sample scenario is as follows. An emergency occurs (e.g., a multiple vehicle accident) on a San Francisco roadway, and one or more persons at the scene who have a SERS app that lists all the services available can request provisions (e.g., defibrillator, medicine, oxygen masks, splints, etc.). Once the Command and Control (CC) receives the request(s), an analysis is made on the number, type, and location of requests to determine the best places (i.e., depots) to deploy their ground service vehicles. For each cluster of requests associated with a depot, a number of rotorcraft will also be deployed to pick up provisions from the depot and drop off the respective provisions.

Model-Based Design (MBD) was used to develop the system, where several different types of models were integrated to deliver the overall system functionality. These models were provided by different stakeholders, involved different types of modeling languages, and supported numerous types of capabilities, such as simulation of real-world scenarios, visualization of vehicles in 2D space, virtual reality interaction with the flight systems atop Google Map of the area, etc., including support for incorporating the physical devices.

3.1   SERS as a Cyber-Physical System

SERS exemplifies the emerging paradigm of Cyber-Physical Systems as ensembles of collaborating embedded software systems [21]. The design of such systems challenges existing approaches for embedded systems such as the V design approach that is common in the aerospace and automotive industry. In the V approach, the system requirements first drive design by a top-down decomposition into subsystems and components, which is then followed by a bottom-up integration into a top-level system. Ultimately, the system integrator is responsible for the end product.

Increasingly, systems are being developed that follow a less rigid design process. These systems comprise systems in their own right and come into existence at runtime. Design and operation of such systems of systems is a challenging endeavor, the success of which is predicated on the use of models across systems, system perspectives, design stages, operational phases, and organizations. SERS serves as an example to highlight some of the key challenges and issues in successfully bringing systems of collaborating systems online.

Figure 4 shows the architecture of SERS [19]. At the core of SERS is Mission Command & Control. As shown along the top of the figure, interaction of emergency personnel with Mission Command & Control takes place via mobile apps, a mission user interface, video stream display, and virtual reality visualization. Along the bottom, devices are shown that communicate with Mission Command & Control and that operate in the physical world. These devices include ground vehicles to set up depots, delivery rotorcraft to deliver provisions in response to aid requests, fixed wing aircraft to provide situational awareness, sensory rotorcraft for use by emergency responders, network rotorcraft to setup an ad hoc network infrastructure [25], a robot arm to provide teleoperated manipulation, a humanoid robot to operate in dangerous environments, and search and rescue dogs with sensory equipment to find survivors and help with damage assessment.

As a reflection of the typical situation for collaborating systems, a broad range of organizations is involved in the design of SERS. These organizations provide expertise in the domains of operations, control, image processing, search and rescue dogs, robotics, communications, networks, and virtual environments.

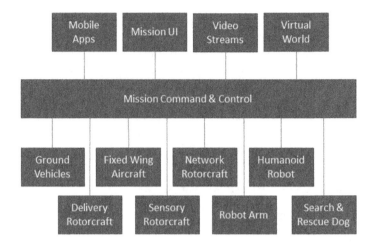

Fig. 4. Architecture of the smart emergency response system

3.2 SERS Design

Figure 5 depicts the SERS elements and their relationships. The overall system synchronizes on time and location. For ground-based entities, location is further restricted to the midpoint of the roads, shown in the lower-left corner of Fig. 5. These midpoints can be retrieved from curated *shape* files from government sites such as the City and County of San Francisco[2].

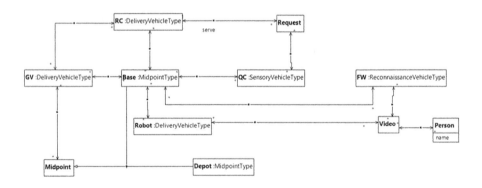

Fig. 5. The elements of SERS

The SERS *Base* station hosts Command & Control and is situated roadside, and is thus attached to a midpoint. Similarly, there are a number of locations (e.g., parks, schools, parking lots, etc.) where the ground vehicles may set up a

---

[2] https://data.sfgov.org/Geographic-Locations-and-Boundaries/Streets-of-San-Francisco-Zipped-Shapefile-Format-/wbm8-ratb.

Depot, so these are also attached to midpoints. Clearly the *ground vehicles* (GV) must be attached to midpoints while they are originally stationed at the base. Each of the ground vehicles is capable of carrying *rotorcraft* (RC) that have a payload carrying capability so that they can deliver provisions to service aid *Requests*. Note that the rotorcraft may also remain stationed at the base. The list of possible provisions to deliver includes a *sensory rotorcraft* (QC) that can stream sensory information such as video from a high definition camera. This video may be streamed back to the Command & Control Center or to a mobile device, for example, operated by a first responder. As the mission unfolds, *fixed-wing aircraft* (FW) embark on *reconnaissance* sorties, for example, to determine the health of the infrastructure. To this end, video may be streamed back to the Command & Control Center as well as to a first responder. Finally, humanoid *Robots* that also support video streaming may be deployed.

In the overall design of SERS, the various elements are represented in many forms using many formalisms. In addition, abstract functionality such as optimizations must be represented. An overview of the range of representations is provided in Fig. 6, where the formalisms used to represent the different elements are attached to these elements with a thick dotted line and shown in gray. The autonomous vehicles are at the center of the overall system and have various representations. In the form of a Computer Aided Design (CAD) model, the structure of the vehicles may be captured. This structure may be stored in a format such as the XML-based *collaborative design activity* (COLLADA) format or a *unified robot description format* (URDF).

From the structural model, a dynamics model of the physics can be automatically generated. Such a model may be represented by a block diagram with continuous time, differential equation, semantics (e.g., a Simulink model). Alternatively, a domain-specific representation such as SimMechanics multibody model may be automatically generated. In addition, a model of the control contributes to the dynamics. The low-level control model may be represented by a block diagram with continuous time or discrete time semantics. There may be different forms of low-level control such as for nominal operation and for system identification purposes. In addition, other forms of control such as supervisory control may be included, which is more appropriately represented by a discrete state formalism such as statecharts.

The models of the different vehicles are identified and calibrated against measurements derived from experiments. The corresponding data is represented in spreadsheets and multi-dimensional tables. Moreover, analysis and validation relies heavily on representation of data as graphs for convenient interpretation and documentation.

For optimization purposes, it is essential to characterize the various vehicles in terms of their longevity, payload, and wind speed. For example, a ground vehicle can set up a depot and operate for days. Rotorcraft, on the other hand, may only be able to fly for 15 min depending on the weight of the payload. Such characterization can be derived from the dynamics models where the data may be captured in the form of a spreadsheet.

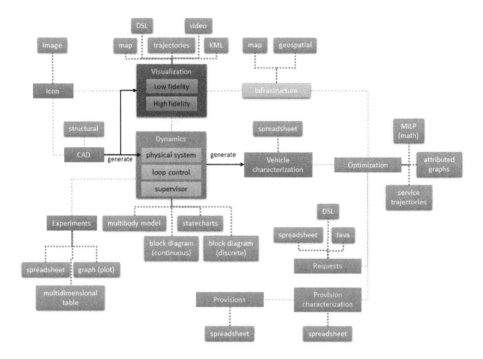

Fig. 6. The various SERS elements and formalisms (gray) used to represent them

Optimization input includes information about the infrastructure in terms of a combination of geospatial (road midpoints) and map information. These two pieces of data provide information as to how ground vehicles can be routed but also where there are potential locations to set up depots.

The remaining input to the optimization relates to the aid requests. First, there is the set of aid requests that come in from either the Command & Control Center or from mobile device apps in the field. To submit the requests, a Java data structure stores request information directly in the mobile device app or a spreadsheet representation may be used to share an underlying mapping. The Command & Control Center, in turn, may rely on a domain-specific language (DSL) to represent the various different requested provisions. Second, for the optimization process, it is necessary to characterize the provisions that can be requested (e.g., how much they weigh), which is information that is represented by a spreadsheet. This characterization is performed for the entire set of provisions, both of which are represented in a spreadsheet.

The optimization itself is then formulated in a mathematical representation. At the foundation are data structures that represent attributed graphs. Specific problems are then solved by using a mixed-integer linear programming (MILP) representation. The result of the optimization is a set of trajectories with service (delivery and pick-up) information attached. Each trajectory is an array of *waypoints* that comprise geospatial data consisting of longitude, latitude, and altitude information as well as dwell time once a waypoint is reached.

A critical aspect of the overall system is visualization to help in design, analysis, test, training, and operation. The Command & Control Center has access to two different types of visualization. In a low fidelity representation, icons that represent the various vehicles are superimposed as images onto a representation of the region as a map. This visualization also shows the different types of aid requests on the map as they come in and at their requested location. The mission trajectories for each of the vehicles as computed by the optimization are also shown in the form of line segments between the waypoints that make up the trajectories. Alternatively, a high-fidelity visualization is available where the vehicles are shown performing their missions as realistic objects (based on the CAD models) in Google Earth as a virtual world. Motion of the objects is shown based on position and orientation information obtained from real-time simulations or physical measurements. Finally, live video data can be streamed to be displayed in the Command & Control Center.

3.3   A Smart Intersection

In a separate project to developing SERS, city planners may wish to install smart intersections that build on vehicle-to-vehicle and vehicle-to-infrastructure technology. A smart intersection system may consist of the elements shown in Fig. 7. The smart intersection system may rely on a *Central Control* unit to coordinate use of the shared intersection surface area. The Central Control unit may have access to the *Streets* that intersect along with the *Traffic* in each of the streets. In addition, the Central Control unit may have access to a *Communication Unit* that allows vehicle-to-infrastructure communication via *communication units* of the *Lights* at the intersection and the *Vehicles* that wish to cross. Both the lights and the vehicle are equipped with a *Control Unit* to implement the functionality necessary to operate as part of a smart intersection. Finally, the central control unit has a network interface to communicate beyond the smart intersection, for example, with city infrastructure monitoring facilities.

3.4   Formalism Integration

At some point in time, the smart intersection infrastructure may wish to be integrated with the SERS. To design an integrated system, a domain-specific formalism would need to account both for the SERS specific elements in Fig. 5 as well as the pertinent smart intersection elements in Fig. 7. These smart intersection elements may include information about the traffic in the streets, and, therefore, only a subset of the smart intersection elements must be integrated with the SERS elements.

SERS involves the integration of at least seven different languages, many of which are domain-specific. Collectively, these languages involve different types of data, different granularity of data, continuous and discrete information, and different levels of abstraction. A wall clock is used to synchronize the activities

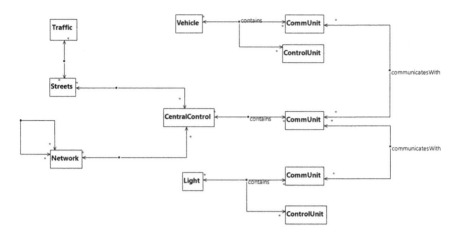

Fig. 7. The elements of a smart intersection

provided by the different components of the system – CAD diagrams, Block
Diagrams (Simulink), Geospatial models, Mixed-Integer Linear Programming
(MILP) models, Android app language, Shape models (map data in terms of
longitude and latitude) and Excel spreadsheets.

4   Research Challenges

The development and analysis of DSMLs has been a research topic for some
time. Thus far, the main focus has been on languages for supporting software
construction in technical domains. There are convincing reasons why the relevance of research on DSMLs will substantially increase in the future. To date,
only a few organizations, even in technical domains, are using DSMLs. Many
domains have not been addressed so far. At the same time, languages and especially DSMLs are at the core of the digital transformation that many societies
and organizations are facing. Among other things, the digital transformation
is characterized by an increasing amount of reality being represented in information systems and by the fact that an ever increasing amount of services is
performed by computers instead of human actors.

Globalization implies the demand for efficiently exchanging information with
systems around the world. As a consequence, there is a need to support the
economic creation and maintenance of application systems as well as their integration. Application systems are linguistic artifacts, i.e., they are constructed
and used through language. DSMLs promise to facilitate the representation of
the domain that is targeted by an application substantially, since they do not
require modelers to build domain-specific concepts from scratch. At the same
time, they promote system integrity, because they, to a certain extent, prevent
inappropriate models from being created. Finally, DSMLs enable the creation of

models that represent complex real world objects and corresponding application systems, thereby empowering users.

The concepts in DSMLs should correspond directly to concepts with which users are familiar. In addition, they should feature a concrete syntax that fosters the intuitive understanding of models. As a consequence, users are not only supported in gaining a better understanding of the systems – and the environment in general – in which they work, but are also enabled to change the respective models and, in turn, the systems they represent. DSMLs also support the efficient exchange of information by allowing the description of complex objects in a more specific way, i.e. with more semantics, thereby substantially reducing the effort and risk caused by the need to reconstruct semantics. In addition to the increased demand for DSMLs, there are various challenges that researchers needs to address to foster the application of DSMLs.

4.1 Software Engineering Challenges Related to the Formal Foundation of Languages

While separation of concerns demands an ever growing number of specialized DSMLs, many use scenarios require the integration of DSMLs. The current state of research includes various promising approaches, however, more challenges remain. Therefore, there is a need for advanced abstractions that enable more sophisticated integration technologies that support the integration or composition of languages and related tools. To take advantage of models during the entire lifecycle of systems (i.e., to support the idea of "models at runtime") future research needs to focus on the integration of modelling tools and application systems. On the one hand, more research on the notorious problem of synchronizing models and code is required, and on the other hand, it requires more research that is aimed at overcoming the principle limitations of current programming languages

Since these languages usually include one classification level only, (meta) classes that are manipulated in respective modelling tools have to be represented as objects on level M0 that creates the need to generate code. Alternatively, programming languages that allow for many classification levels would enable a common representation of models and code. With respect to maintaining DSMLs or family of DSMLs, powerful abstraction concepts are essential. Languages that focus on static information already have support for various abstraction concepts such as classification or generalization/specialization. Unfortunately, this is not the case for process modelling languages. These languages present a specific research challenge because dynamic abstractions are an obstacle to monotonic extensions, i.e., they do not allow a straightforward enforcement of the substitutability constraint [17]. Existing approaches that focus on relaxed versions of the substitutability constraint (e.g. [5,23]) are insufficient, because they depend on premises that often cannot be satisfied.

4.2   Challenges Related to the (Re-) Construction of Domain-Specific Concepts

The construction of DSMLs cannot be restricted to their formal properties. Instead, they are intended to provide domain-specific concepts, the (re-) construction of which is not trivial. At the same time, it is usually not an option to leave this part of DSML development to domain experts, because they lack the knowledge required to develop appropriate abstractions. Against this background, future research on DSMLs has to take into account the peculiarities of reconstructing domain-specific concepts.

Methods that Support the Development of DSMLs. Existing methods for requirements analysis and system development are only partially suited to support the development of DSMLs. With respect to analyzing requirements, there is the problem that prospective users often lack a sufficient understanding of the artifact to be developed. In other words, they do not know what to expect. Hence, respective methods need to support users in developing a clearer picture of a DSML and/or the functionality it may provide. With respect to designing a DSML, methods should provide guidance for supporting various challenging decisions (see below). Research on specific methods for DSML development has recently emerged (e.g. [10]).

Distinguishing Between a Language and Its Application. The technical terms found in a domain are candidates for being included in a respective DSML. However, not all of them are suited for that purpose. The decision of whether a concept should be part of a DSML or should rather be specified with that DSML can be a remarkable challenge. The following example concepts illustrate this challenge: "Document", "Goal", "Product", "Risk", "ERP System", "Department". It is conceivable that all of these concepts are part of a DSML or can be defined using a DSML. Even though this decision depends on the specifics of a given case, it also depends on general criteria that have not been investigated sufficiently. They relate to economic and epistemological concerns.

Economics of DSMLs. The design of a DSML presents a fundamental economic challenge. On the one hand, a DSML should promote modelling productivity. For this reason it should provide specific concepts that fit the particular requirements of a domain. In other words, the concepts should reflect a high degree of domain-specific semantics (in the sense of information content). On the other hand, a DSML should enable a wide range of reuse in order to promote economies of scale. For this purpose, it should be built from concepts that abstract from specific features of domains. Since both objectives are of pivotal relevance for the economics of DSML and, as a consequence, for their use in practice, this conflict creates a research challenge that should be addressed. Figure 8 illustrates the problem.

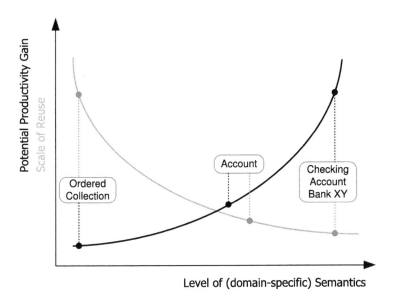

Fig. 8. Illustration of DSML design conflict

Note that the gradients of the curve will usually not be known precisely. The two example concepts show how the apparent conflict can be relaxed by including concepts on a higher level of abstraction (such as "Organizational Unit") that can be further refined to more specific needs (e.g. "University Department"). This situation reveals two research challenges. First there is the need to structure DSMLs into high level ("textbook") concepts and more specific ones that are tuned to narrower domains. Second, the semantics of the required refinement has to be specified. This is not a trivial task, since in many cases neither specialization nor inheritance alone is sufficient. Figure 9 illustrates this challenge. It represents concepts to model products. While the level of abstraction is apparently increasing from the bottom to the top, the relationships between the levels seem to combine characteristics of instantiation and specialization, which creates a serious problem, since there is a strict dichotomy between both refinement operations.

A further aspect of the above trade-off is related to standardization. With respect to the use of DSMLs, standardization is of pivotal relevance. It contributes to the protection of investments, fosters the dissemination of languages and, hence, economies of scale. Furthermore, decision makers appreciate standardization because it provides legitimization. However, standardization has a severe downside – it freezes a certain state and, because of the benefits it provides, creates a substantial obstacle to progress. Research on DSMLs can hardly ignore this conflict and therefore needs to aim at abstractions that are suited to develop standards that are open for evolution.

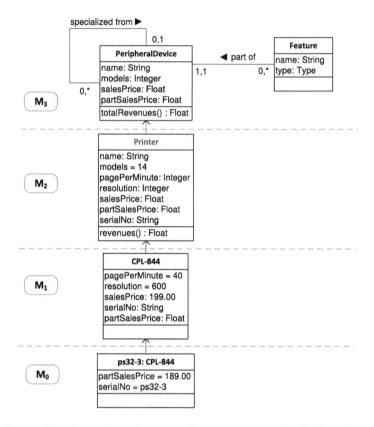

Fig. 9. Illustration of stepwise refinement of concepts over multiple classification levels

Top-Down Versus Bottom-Up Development. To effectively address the conflicts outlined above it seems most promising to develop DSMLs in a top-down approach. That would allow similarities between different domains to be exploited. As a consequence, a top-down approach would be especially promising with respect to reuse and integration of languages. However, it is unrealistic to assume that existing languages can be easily replaced – people are accustomed to them and investments need to be protected. Therefore, research should focus on approaches that are suitable for combining aspects of top-down approaches with those of bottom-up approaches.

Epistemology of DSML Design. Designing DSMLs for global use has to account for remarkable conceptual diversity. The technical languages used in certain related communities around the world not only vary with respect to designators, but also with respect to the semantics of concepts. From an epistemological perspective, there are two extreme interpretations of this conceptual diversity. On the one hand, one may assume that particular domains are actually different with respect to relevant objects, tasks, constraints etc. In that case, the diversity of technical languages would simply reflect ontological diversity and has to be accepted. On the other hand, one may regard conceptual diversity as the result of a cultural evolution that is characterized by chance and arbitrariness. Hence, actual technical languages are a contingent matter – they could be different and still serve their purpose. There is evidence for the latter assumption. The widespread use of ERP systems shows that organizations are able to adapt to a certain common conceptual foundation. As a consequence of this assumption, diversity could be reduced by proposing DSMLs that replace existing concepts with new ones in order to enable unified domains of discourse. While these considerations seem to be of a philosophical nature only, they are actually highly relevant for the design of DSMLs. They imply that it may not be sufficient to reconstruct the actual use of technical languages, but to ask whether they are appropriate and how conceptual diversity can be overcome.

Quality of DSMLs. If we follow Kant, who claims there is no recognition without concepts [16], and furthermore accept that certain concepts are more or less suited to structure a domain of interest with respect to a given purpose, then the construction of a DSML should not just aim at representing existing concepts, but eventually at reconstructing them with the intention to making them a better instrument for modeling. This corresponds to what Richard Rorty demanded for Philosophy – "Philosophers have long wanted to understand concepts, but the point is to change them so as to make them serve our purposes better." [22]. As a consequence, research on DSMLs needs to develop an elaborate, multi-perspective notion of language quality that not only comprises formal aspects, but also accounts for domain-specific concepts as well as for economic and cognitive aspects (for a respective approach see [10]).

Support for Language Evolution. The world is going to change. However, we lack powerful theories that would allow for comprehensive predictions. As a consequence, it seems unavoidable that DSMLs have to be adapted from time to time. Therefore, future research needs to aim at supporting language evolution, including abstractions as well as respective tools that foster flexibility. Furthermore, the organization of the evolution is essential – should it be a managed process or would an agile approach be more suitable? What kind of incentives could be built to motivate stakeholders to contribute to language evolution and to migrate to new language versions.

Accounting for Cultural Challenges. The success of a DSML not only depends on its quality, it also depends on economic and political decisions that enable its use and dissemination. However, neither in organizations nor in the public is there sufficient awareness of the pivotal relevance of languages in general, and DSMLs in particular, for managing the digital transformation. As a consequence, funding for respective research projects remains relatively limited and organizations are reluctant to invest in language technologies. If research on DSMLs is seriously interested in practical impact, it cannot ignore these obstacles. Instead, we need to put more emphasis on clarifying the tremendous economic and societal relevance of designing and disseminating DSMLs. This also includes the revision of university curricula.

Organization of Research. The development of DSMLs and related tools requires substantial effort. That is even more so if one aims at languages and tools that should be disseminated in practice. Most research institutions, especially those in academia, do not have the resources to accomplish this objective on their own. This would require not only bundling of resources, but would also require the involved groups to agree on common concepts. Unfortunately, such an approach would contradict a core characteristic of scientific research – in order to promote progress, researchers are supposed to compete and challenge their peers. This conflict has to be taken into consideration.

4.3 Thoughts on Possible Future Directions to Pursue

The above considerations are intended to point at gaps in the state of the art that future research might address. Finally, we consider a few promising approaches for addressing selected challenges.

Multilevel Language Architectures. Traditional approaches to conceptual modeling are based on two classification levels: The M2 layer is used to define the metamodel of a modeling language and the M1 layer serves to represent corresponding models. However, such a language architecture is insufficient since it does not address the pivotal conflict of designing DSMLs – that is, it is not possible to specify a generic DSML that is subsequently refined into more specific ones, thereby supporting both a wide range of reuse (on the more generic level) and high productivity of reuse (on more specific levels). Multilevel language architectures that enable an arbitrary number of classification levels [6] and support "deep instantiation" [7,11] address this problem.

However, current programming languages that feature one classification level only prevent a tight integration of models and respective application systems at runtime. Elements of conceptual models, even though located conceptually at M1 or higher have to be represented within a tool at the M0 level. As a consequence, they cannot be further instantiated, which makes it mandatory to keep code and models in separate representations resulting in the notorious problem of synchronizing code and models. Programming languages that allow for multiple levels of classification, such as those that are based on the "golden braid" architecture [8] allow models to be represented at the intended level of classification and, as a consequence, allow for a common representation of models and code.

Establishing "Open Model" Communities. The effort required to develop an elaborate DSML is not only beyond the capabilities of single research institutions, it also demands the involvement of stakeholders from practice, such as prospective users and tool vendors. At the same time, it seems reasonable to demand that DSMLs should be available to everybody in order to promote their dissemination and further development. Against this background, it seems promising to take the open source software initiative (which has been impressively successful in places) as a model for building similar communities that focus on the joint development and dissemination of DSMLs and respective models. Respective initiatives could also aim at fostering collaboration between various disciplines that are required to develop DSMLs. Furthermore, they can be seen as a new model for organizing research following the ideas of open science [13] and as a catalyst for disseminating research results to business practice. Early attempts to establish "open model" communities [9,12] indicate that it is crucial to account for building effective incentives for participation, both for academics and practitioners.

Raising Awareness. In various disciplines such as Philosophy, Psychology, and Sociology, the recognition that language is of pivotal relevance for almost all investigations resulted in "linguistic turns". As a consequence, the awareness for the foundational role of language has considerably grown in these disciplines. In Computer Science, language has always been a key foundation, especially formal languages and programming languages. However, with respect to the development of DSMLs, there is a need to increase the awareness of content, i.e. the relevance of reconstructing domain-specific concepts, which clearly requires to climb over the "firewall" that Dijkstra suggested. In addition to that, it will be important to start campaigns that aim at convincing funding agencies and politicians that artificial languages are not just a marginal instrument for promoting automation, but lie at the core of the digital world and will thus play a crucial and essential role in our future lives.

References

1. http://research.microsoft.com/en-us/projects/formula/
2. www.porticoproject.org
3. https://wiki.isis.vanderbilt.edu/OpenC2WT/index.php/Main_Page
4. IEEE Standard for Modeling and Simulation (M&S) High Level Architecture (HLA) - Framework and Rules. IEEE Std. 1516–2000, pp. i–22 (2000)
5. van der Aalst, W.M.P., Basten, T.: Inheritance of workflows: An approach to tackling problems related to change. Theo. Comput. Sci. **270**(1–2), 125–203 (2002)
6. Atkinson, C., Kühne, T.: The essence of multilevel metamodeling. In: Gogolla, M., Kobryn, C. (eds.) UML 2001. LNCS, vol. 2185, pp. 19–33. Springer, Heidelberg (2001)
7. Atkinson, C., Kühne, T.: Reducing accidental complexity in domain models. Soft. Syst. Model. **7**(3), 345–359 (2008)
8. Clark, T., Sammut, P., Willans, J.: Applied metamodelling: a foundation for language driven development. Ceteva, 2nd edn. (2008)
9. France, R.B., Bieman, J., Cheng, B.H.C.: Repository for Model Driven Development (ReMoDD). In: Kühne, T. (ed.) MoDELS 2006. LNCS, vol. 4364, pp. 311–317. Springer, Heidelberg (2007)

10. Frank, U.: Domain-specific modeling languages - requirements analysis and design guidelines. In: Reinhartz-Berger, I., Sturm, A., Clark, T., Wand, Y., Cohen, S., Bettin, J. (eds.) Domain Engineering: Product Lines, Conceptual Models, and Languages, pp. 133–157. Springer (2013)
11. Frank, U.: Multilevel modeling: toward a new paradigm of conceptual modeling and information systems design. Bus. Inf. Syst. Eng. **6**(6), 319–337 (2014)
12. Frank, U., Strecker, S.: Open reference models - community-driven collaboration to promote development and dissemination of reference models. Enterp. Model. Inf. Syst. Architect. **2**(2), 32–41 (2007)
13. Guadamuz, A.L.: Open science: Open source licences in scientific research. North Carolina J. Law Technol. **7**(2), 321–366 (2006)
14. Hemingway, G., Neema, H., Nine, H., Sztipanovits, J., Karsai, G.: Rapid synthesis of high-level architecture-based heterogeneous simulation: a model-based integration approach. Simulation, page 0037549711401950 (2011)
15. Jackson, E., Porter, P., Sztipanovits, J.: Semantics of domain specific modeling languages. In: Mosterman, P.J., Nicolescu, G. (eds.) Model-Based Design of Heterogeneous Embedded Systems, pp. 437–486 (2009)
16. Kant, I.: Critique of Pure Reason. Penguin Classics (2007)
17. Liskov, B.H., Wing, J.M.: A behavioral notion of subtyping. ACM Trans. Program. Lang. Syst. **16**, 1811–1841 (1994)
18. Mosterman, P.J., Sanabria, D.E., Bilgin, E., Zhang, K., Zander, J.: A heterogeneous fleet of vehicles for automated humanitarian missions. Comput. Sci. Eng. **12**, 90–95 (2014)
19. Mosterman, P.J., Sanabria, D.E., Bilgin, E., Zhang, K., Zander, J.: Automating humanitarian missions with a heterogeneous fleet of vehicles. Ann. Rev. Control **38**(2), 259–270 (2014)
20. Mosterman, P.J., Sanabria, D.E., Bilgin, E., Zhang, K., Zander, J.: A heterogeneous fleet of vehicles for automated humanitarian missions. Comput. Sci. Eng. **16**(3), 90–95 (2014)
21. Mosterman, P.J., Zander, J.: Cyber-physical systems challenges–a needs analysis for collaborating embedded software systems. Softw. Syst. Model. **15**(1), 1–12 (2016). (in press)
22. Rorty, R.: Universality and truth. In: Brandom, R.B. (ed.) Rorty and His Critics, pp. 1–30. Blackwell Publishing Ltd., Malden, MA and Oxford and Carlton (2000)
23. Schrefl, M., Stumptner, M.: Behavior-consistent specialization of object life cycles. ACM Trans. Softw. Eng. Methodol. **11**(1), 92–148 (2002)
24. Simko, G., Lindecker, D., Levendovszky, T., Neema, S., Sztipanovits, J.: Specification of cyber-physical components with formal semantics – integration and composition. In: Moreira, A., Schätz, B., Gray, J., Vallecillo, A., Clarke, P. (eds.) MODELS 2013. LNCS, vol. 8107, pp. 471–487. Springer, Heidelberg (2013)
25. Wan, Y., Shengli, F., Zander, J., Mosterman, P.J.: Transforming on-demand emergency communication: Needs, analyses, and solutions. Homel. Secur. Today **11**(9), 32–35 (2015)
26. Zander, J., Mosterman, P.J.: Model-based design of a smart emergency response system. Design News (2014)

Globalized Domain Specific Language Engineering

Barrett Bryant[1], Jean-Marc Jézéquel[2], Ralf Lämmel[3], Marjan Mernik[4],
Martin Schindler[5], Friedrich Steinmann[6], Juha-Pekka Tolvanen[7(✉)],
Antonio Vallecillo[8], and Markus Völter[9]

[1] University of North Texas, Denton, USA
[2] University of Rennes, Rennes, France
Jean-Marc.Jezequel@irisa.fr
[3] University of Koblenz-Landau, Koblenz, Germany
[4] University of Maribor, Maribor, Slovenia
[5] MaibornWolff GmbH, Munich, Germany
[6] FernUniversität in Hagen, Hagen, Germany
[7] MetaCase, Jyväskylä, Finland
jpt@metacase.com
[8] University of Málaga, Málaga, Spain
[9] Independent/itemis, Stuttgart, Germany

Abstract. This chapter is dedicated to discussing the engineering
aspects involved in the integration of modeling languages, as an essential
part of the globalization process. It covers the foundations of language
integration, the definition of the relationships between the languages to
be integrated, and the various dimensions of language and tool integration. Language variants, evolution, refactoring and retirement are also
discussed, as key issues involved in the globalization of modeling languages.

Keywords: Globalized DSLs · Language Engineering

1 Problem Statement

Today's software development is characterized by a large degree of improvisa-
tion: different languages and language-based tools are used to create different
artifacts that act on the same (physical or logical) system. Such multiplicity
is not a problem in itself, but rather the common situation of those languages
and tools to be insufficiently integrated. The languages and tools though involve
interaction at the system level and these interactions are hard to understand
without good integration. In fact, the actual interactions may disagree with the
intended interactions. Any analysis or verification is going to be hard. Excessive
testing may be needed and still fail to be conclusive.

We just may hope for the engineers collaborating on the same system to limit
themselves to a set of languages implemented with a single language workbench.
Version changes of languages and tools would be semantics preserving (both

© Springer International Publishing Switzerland 2015
B.H.C. Cheng et al. (Eds.): Globalizing Domain-Specific Languages, LNCS 9400, pp. 43–69, 2015.
DOI: 10.1007/978-3-319-26172-0_4

backwards and forward compatible) and therefore not require any changes to the current artifacts.

Clearly, this is impractical. One issue is that engineers need to use multiple languages to deal with different concerns. This poses the obvious problems of *co-reference*, as illustrated by several motivating examples given in Sect. 2 of this chapter.

The assumption of a single version or forward and backward compatible evolution is too limiting, also. As teams grow bigger, different tools, different versions or variants of the same language or tool will be used by different engineers even for the same DSL. Even if the different tools allow the interchange of artifacts, there is no guarantee that the semantics are preserved. Even if a new version of a tool is fully backward compatible, it is usually not forward compatible, creating an impediment if some engineers continue using the old tools.

Beyond the pure exchange of *prodels*[1] as a whole, tools may be used to refine or extend prodels created by another tool; tools may also need to collaborate on some prodels. Even if the interfaces for refinement, extension, and access of prodels are explicitly defined (which is trivially the case for single-language prodels), the (full) semantics is usually implicit in the tool itself. Practically, this leads to a combined tool whose behavior is difficult to predict, leading to largely unforeseeable outcomes.

This chapter is dedicated to discussing the engineering aspects involved in the integration of modeling languages, as an essential part of the globalization process. It covers the definition of the relationships between the languages to be integrated (and/or their corresponding prodels), exploring the different dimensions of correspondence in Sect. 3. Then, Sect. 4 discusses the state of the art in domain-specific programming and modeling languages, with particular emphasis on the foundations of language integration. In Sect. 5, the various dimensions of language and tool integration are elaborated. Section 6 addresses the specific case of language variants and Sect. 7 addresses language evolution, refactoring, and retirement.

2   Motivating Examples

2.1   Complementary City Maps

A city is a complex system involving many kinds of concerns: road network, transportation systems, water and electricity conductions, orography, geomorphology, and others. Capturing all the associated data in a single map would be impossible or useless. Instead, different maps are used, each one focusing on a different concern and purpose. Thus, each kind of map gives rise to a designated DSL and there is clearly an integration requirement in how all the different maps need to be consistent with each other.

Any given map applies a specific abstraction to reality. For instance, the relative distance between city locations may or may not be preserved by a specific map. Almost a century ago (in 1931) the first diagrammatic map of

---

[1] We use the term "prodel" to refer to either programs or models.

London's rapid transit network was designed by Harry Beck, who invented a new language that permitted drawing schematic diagrams, not showing the geographic locations but rather the relative positions of the stations, lines, the stations' connective relations, and fare zones. Such a map should then be used with other city maps, like the one showing the streets, for reasoning about possible routes or for deciding alternative paths. The integration between them takes place in the head of the person reading them, and the correspondence between their elements is implicit, based on the names of the tube stations that appear in both maps. The names then make a *common frame of reference*.

2.2 House Building

Building a house involves many trades, including bricklaying, plumbing, and electrical engineering. Each of these trades has its own rules (expressing constraints) and its own (graphical) languages.

To a certain extent, each trade can design its deliverable independently of the others. Some requirements of the building (e.g., size, number of rooms, classification of rooms) are global and hence shared between all trades, others (e.g., which rooms need an ethernet plug) are local (i.e., specific to a trade). Each trade must thus design its deliverable to meet global and local constraints.

Some of the global constraints may imply interaction (coordination) between trades. For instance, the number of slots in the walls of a building, horizontal ones especially, is usually to be kept to a minimum. Plumbing and electrical engineering therefore need to share slots, which are to be created by the bricklayers. The length of the pipes and cables required depends on where the slots are and, reversely, the slots are best placed so that the used material (or loss of energy) is minimized. At this point, the trades can no longer work independently; their designs rely on a *shared frame of reference*. Since house construction is a material matter, one such joint frame of reference is position in space.

The use of a joint frame of reference may be carried out in an ad-hoc manner, e.g., by attaching notes; note how this corresponds to adding comments or annotations to a program. Alternatively, the underlying languages may support a common frame of reference through designated language constructs. If the integration is ad-hoc (improvised), it escapes formal analysis, and design errors will not be detected.

2.3 The A380 Wiring Issue

When the first physical prototype of the A380 was assembled, it was found that some of the electrical wires and harnesses were too short, even though they had been manufactured to their specification. One reason for this, it was identified that the engineers designing the body of the aircraft had upgraded to a newer version of the jointly used CAD software, while the engineers designing the wiring still used the old version. This prevented the latter from automatically integrating design changes they made to the wiring into the 3D model of the aircraft, and also from automatically adapting the wiring to design changes made to the body. The workarounds used by engineers to integrate their data nevertheless were imperfect, hence the failure.

While from a technical viewpoint, the reasons for the failure appear to be clear (as do the measures that would have been necessary to avoid the failure, namely the use of the same CAD version), it is a fact of life that engineers are reluctant to change their tools, and hence changes midway through a project are difficult to accomplish. Changes would not be necessary if the version change had been engineered with globalization in mind.

2.4   Tool Bug Fixes

Often enough, engineers will discover bugs in the tools they use. Sometimes, working around these bugs (for instance, by negating a condition that is obviously interpreted the wrong way, or by adding 1 to an expression to fix an off-by-one error) is easier than getting the bugs fixed. However, when the tool does get fixed, the fixed-by-workaround prodels will break. Ideally, this would be automatically discovered by a globalized prodeling tool.

3   Basic Notions of Language Integration

3.1   Correspondences by Level

In many cases of complex systems the globalization of languages manifests itself today on the fact that prodels written in completely independent languages refer to the same system (red arrows in Fig. 1), or more exactly to different aspects of it.

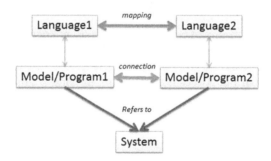

Fig. 1. Correspondences between layers at different levels (Color figure online).

If these aspects are completely independent, or orthogonal, then there is no particular problem in doing this. The trouble appears as soon as someone realizes that these aspects need to interact or do interact in perhaps ways that are not fully understood at a given point in time, for example competition for the same set of (computational or physical) resources or the heat generated by a computation and its speed. Then there is a need to relate the two corresponding models M1 and M2 through some form of connection (orange arrow). The next stage is to do it at the language level, by defining a relation (e.g., intersection, maybe union, maybe a form of composition) between Language1 and Language2 syntactic and semantic domains (blue arrow).

Of course relating languages with such a blue arrow would give for free the orange connection between models, and allow much more powerful reasoning capacities on the System.

3.2   Language Relationships

Not all languages are developed independently from each other. Instead a new language might be developed based on an existing language. Additionally, languages are often not stable but evolve over time. Each of these resulting languages can be seen as a separate language but are also related to each other. To clearly distinguish these different relationships between languages we use the following definitions within this document:

Variant: Language variants are different languages used for similar purposes within the same domain, and thus typically sharing a common semantic domain. For instance Fig. 2 provides a simple example of a language variant. It shows a very basic metamodel for a state machine language, while Fig. 3 provides a variant of it allowing the concept of hierarchical state machine by having the class StateMachine inheriting from State. The second one can be seen as a dialect of the first one. These languages co-exist and can be used more or less interchangeably.

Version: Language versions are actually the same language which evolved over time, for instance the language of Fig. 3 could also be seen as an evolution of the one of Fig. 2. Usually these languages are used in sequence within the same project scope, which might introduce forward and backwards compatibilities issue (see Sect. 5.3).

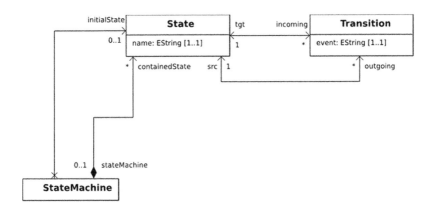

Fig. 2. Language variant 1: Meta-model of a state machine.

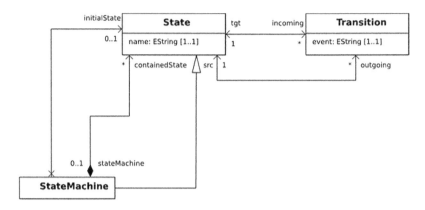

Fig. 3. Language variant 2: Meta-model of a hierarchical state machine.

Viewpoint: Viewpoint languages are different languages within the same domain to describe different aspects or concerns of the system, e.g., structure and behavior, whereas one viewpoint can cover more than one concern. Usually these viewpoints share some concepts within the domain or might have some overlapping in the described concerns of the system.

Composition: A composition is a collection of languages with a defined semantic relationship between each other. The relationship might be either defined by references between the languages keeping the prodels separately (language family) or by embedding one language into another one (language extension; see Sect. 4). Usually the languages in the family or the composite language are variants or concerns.

These language relationships might be either coordinated or uncoordinated. Language versions are usually created by language evolution by adding, replacing, or removing language constructs within an existing language. This is considered as a coordinated relationship between the old and the new version of the language as the evolution is done on an intentional basis. On the other side variants can occur independently from each other allowing to express the same aspects of the system with different notations or concepts. This is considered as an uncoordinated relationship if this happened unintentionally.

Language versions also raise the question of compatibility (backward and forward) and migration of legacy prodels which are discussed in Sects. 5.3 and 7, respectively.

3.3   Frames of Reference

In order to control the interaction (both direct and indirect, via the system) between prodels, correspondences (cf. Sect. 5.4) must be established. One way of expressing correspondence is by using common frames of reference.

Explicit Frames of Reference. An explicit frame of reference provides an agreed common representation of the entities that are the subject of the prodels. These entities could be

- memory locations (i.e., objects on the heap)
- records in a database
- Uniform Resource Identifiers (URIs)
- part numbers or RFID tags (in physical systems)

Jointly using these representations allows coordination at the artifact level. Each language has to encompass a way of addressing the representations.

Explicit frames of reference are characterized by the occurrence of explicit references in the prodels that use them. Although these references can be ad hoc (using comments, notes, etc.), it is preferable that the used prodeling language provide for them. This in turn means that the language must subscribe to the shared frame of reference as well. Thus, using explicit frames of reference, languages should not be developed entirely independently from each other.

For languages built on a common language infrastructure, the language interoperability interface provides a common frame of reference that is adopted by all participating languages. Here, prodels can refer to elements of prodels in other languages directly. One example of such an explicit frame of reference is the CLI standard[2], which basically builds on types in the object-oriented sense. The Microsoft Component Object Model (COM) is another example of a standardized joint frame of reference.

Implicit Frames of Reference. A shared frame of reference may also be established after the fact. For instance, by analysing a set of different language prodels, the joint use of same or similar names may suggest that same entities are referenced in different prodels. For instance, a tube map and a street map may not use (refer to) the same tube stations explicitly, and yet, the names of tube stations can often be mapped to the names of streets or places, establishing an implicit frame of reference. Another, more technical example is that of AspectJ: here, a pointcut language is used to specify places in (arbitrary) prodels at which advice is invoked.

The risk of using implicit frames of reference is that their existence is not made explicit to the stakeholders (meaning that collaborating parties are not aware of the fact that something is implicit/happening implicitly). On the other hand, implicit frames of reference are more flexible, as they allow interoperability without an upfront grand design. A good balance between implicit and explicit frames of reference can be struck by lifting the mechanisms used to identify the implicit frames of reference at runtime to design time, where they can be marked in the prodels. Again, AspectJ with its so-called join point shadows may serve as an example here.

---

[2] http://en.wikipedia.org/wiki/Common_Language_Infrastructure.

Engineering Frames of Reference. Names usually refer to objects. A common frame of reference that uses names therefore usually uses objects, and hence shared state, as the pivots of prodel interaction. Shared state is a problem if a state change caused by one prodel causes inconsistency of another prodel, for instance since it violates an invariant. One way to handle this is to push the common frame of reference to a special environment which guarantees that invariants from all prodels using it are always maintained. A good example of such an external environment is a database.

Things get much more complicated, however, if the frame of reference uses other notions, such as behaviour. In fact, when the prodeling paradigms which require the common frame of reference do not match (which is, for instance, the case when a system is prodeled using differential equations and UML), engineering a common frame of reference may be a major engineering effort.

4   Approaches to Language Composition

Language composition is, together with interoperability and collaboration, the third possibility of interaction among heterogeneous modeling languages for achieving globalization. The goal is to build a language simply by reusing different language definition modules (fragments), such as modules for expressions, declarations, and afterwards straightforwardly extend them to reflect language design changes. This was indeed achieved to some extend using single a formalism and a language workbench. Recently, a taxonomy of language compositions has been proposed [6]; it was also recognized that language composability is not a property of languages themselves, but a property of language definitions. To enable language composition, a language module (fragment) has to be reused as is; that is, any changes to a language module (fragment) are not allowed, but new language modules (fragments) can be added that extend or override previous language modules (fragments). In other words, only non-invasive changes of previous language modules (fragments) are allowed in language composition. Four different types of language composition have been identified in [6]:

- In **language extension** $(B \lhd E)$, the definition of base language B (a dominant language) is extended with a new language module (fragment) E. Note, that in this case language module (fragment) E makes little sense when regarded independently from the base language B. This type of language composition also subsumes **language restriction** (a language module (fragment) E can remove some features from the language).
- In **language unification** $(L1 \uplus L2)$, two languages $L1$ and $L2$ are composed together by writing glue code g. Dominance of one language over another does not exist (as is the case in language extension) and both language definitions are complete and stand alone.
- In **self-extension** $(H \leftarrow E)$, the language definition does not change. The host language H is powerful enough that new extensions E can be implemented using macros, templates, function composition, operator overloading,

or libraries that provide domain-specific constructs. This form of language composition is also called pure language embedding [15].

– In **extension composition**, the language definitions are composed using previous language compositions that show how different compositions can work together. An examples of extension composition is $(L1 \uplus L2) \triangleleft L3$.

Another dimension of language composition is whether a language definition is informal (language syntax and semantics are hard-coded in compiler or interpreter), formal (syntax and semantics are formally specified with one of several formal methods for language definition), or semi-formal (syntax is formally specified, but semantics is not). As we can expect different forms of language compositions are much harder to achieve when syntax and/or semantics are only informally specified [21].

Globalization of modeling languages requires interaction of heterogenous modeling languages, which are designed and developed using different formalisms and different language workbenches. In this case a language composition is even harder to achieve since we would like to reuse language modules (fragements) written in different formalism and developed possibly in different language workbenches. On the other hand, semantics of modeling languages are often only informally specified making a language composition more difficult. Some open problems in language composition with respect to globalization of modeling languages are:

– How to obtain fully modular, extensible, and reusable modeling language definitions, which can be combined despite developed using different formalisms and language workbenches?
– Can various forms of language composition be achieved not only at syntax level (using different formalisms and tools for describing a syntax), but also at the semantic level?
– Can language interfaces (Chap. 1) help us in language composition?
– How to change accompanying tools after language composition? Can such tools be automatically generated?

5   Dimensions for Language and Tool Integration

The composition of two languages can come in two very different flavors: the first flavor is that a language is explicitly designed to compose with (e.g., extend) another one. In the second case, two (or more) languages that have been designed independently are composed. While in the first case the semantics can be aligned, the second case may lead to unexpected semantic interactions (this is an example of the well-know feature interaction problem). It is currently an unresolved challenge to reason about the composition of independently developed languages and avoid unexpected interactions.

5.1   Referencing/Explicit Frames of Reference (Based on the Same Infrastructure/Meta Meta Model)

Name References. The simplest form of language integration is name references. A model element in model M1 (expressed in language L1) references a symbol by name that is defined in M2 (expressed in L2). The reference is really just a name, with no direct IDE support, (because we cannot modify the tools to provide the IDE support or the target model is not available). This means that no technical integration between the two tools (for authoring L1 and L2 models) is necessary. Of course, this approach is very error-prone, so in practice, one often builds third-party checking tools where, for example, the two models M2 and M1 are exported and the name references are checked for consistency relative to the names defined in M2. The user experience is, however, not very convenient because no real-time support is available for the user when using names that are (supposedly) defined in M2.

Tool-Supported Name References. An improvement over pure name references are tool-supported name references. Specifically this means that as the user authors M2, he can use code completion (or some other means of selection) to select any of the existing names in M1. Also, names used in M2 that are not defined in M1 are flagged as an error, directly in the tool. While this approach is obviously more convenient and less error-prone, it is harder to achieve because the two authoring tools for L1 and L2 (called T1 and T2, respectively) have to be changed:

– If T2 provides an API to query the model, then T1 must be changed to call this API if the user enters a name (or during name validation). While this approach is nice in that it provides real-time integration, the drawback is that T2 has to run for T1 to be able to call the service.
– T1 may load the T2 prodel file and extract the valid names from the model. This requires no change to T2, but requires changes to T1. The advantage is that T2 does not have to be running while T1 is used. A related approach is that T2 exports some kind of file that is dedicated to the collaboration.

Real References. Option 2 already feels like a tight integration from a user's perspective. However, as we have discussed in (2), this may require significant efforts in terms of changing the two tools. A better solution is to build both tools on top of the same platform (meta meta model). Today this is often Eclipse EMF Ecore. Once this is done, references in L2 can be actual references to concepts defined in L1 – the two meta models are directly related. Of course this requires L2 to be aware of L1: when L2 is built, L1 has to be available to the developer so he can define the reference. However, once this is done, establishing the references (e.g., via code completion) and checking referential integrity) becomes simple and is supported by the EMF infrastructure.

5.2   Language Embedding

From the point of view of language integration, Fowler [9] has classified Domain-Specific Languages as internal and external. An external DSL is distinct from the host language, typically doesn't share any data structures, and often merely provides an API through which the DSL operations may be invoked by the host language. Java Database Connectivity (JDBC) [25] is a typical example of this, where SQL [26] statements are passed as strings to the SQL interpreter to be executed, returning the results of queries in a Java data structure.

A domain-specific language is said to be embedded if it is integrated into a host language, often a general-purpose programming language [31], but it could also be the case that two or more DSLs are unified [6]. The notion of embedding corresponds to Fowler's internal DSL. Internal DSLs may be further classified as shallow embedded or deeply embedded [12]. Shallow embedded DSLs, while appearing to be extensions of the host language, restrict their interaction to returning values that the host language program may use. Embedded SQL [23] is an example of this. SQL code appears in the host language program directly and serves to return values, which are then used by the host language program. In contrast, a language extension such as SQLJ [24], which extends Java with SQL, is designed to operate much more seamlessly in the Java environment as opposed to having its own separate implementation. Such language extension is discussed in more detail in the next section.

Deeply embedded DSL code creates an abstract syntax tree (AST), which may then be integrated directly into the host language program, and even manipulated by that program. In effect, this allows the DSL code to itself be a first-class object, as opposed to just the value it computes being the first-class object (i.e., shallow embedding). This approach has been efficiently developed in languages such as Haskell [15] and Scala [11], which have rich type systems capable of representing such embedded DSL code. In particular, the use of Haskell as a meta-language for defining the semantics of DSLs has become widespread (e.g., see [8]). Hudak [15] points out that this type of language unification allows for a well-defined "domain semantics" of the DSL, which is defined by an interpreter for the ASTs, and is separate from the semantics of the host language. On the other hand, the DSL can reuse an underlying programming language infrastructure [14,18]. Furthermore, such embedded DSLs are easier to compose than DSLs implemented by direct translation into the host language [5,22].

All of the above discussion has been concerned with Domain-Specific Languages. There are some other issues to be considered when considering Domain-Specific Modeling Languages (DSMLs), even though the difference between the two is subtle [33]. Fritzsche et al. [10] discuss the syntactic and semantic differences between embedded DSLs and embedded DSMLs. A fundamental one is that while DSLs must have their semantics fully defined to be executable, a DSML may still be useful without a complete semantics. From an implementation point of view, an embedded DSML model may be integrated with the host model via model transformation.

5.3   Language Extension (Adding New Language Constructs)

Intuitively speaking, extending a language is adding new language constructs to it – of course, in a modular (non-invasive) way. That turns into adding new model elements into its meta-model, be it new classes, new attributes or new associations or inheritance links. Language extensions occur routinely when a new (backwards compatible) language version with new features is released. The prototypical example of this is the Java programming language.

But of course adding concepts to the meta-model is not enough. In most of the cases, it will also have impact on the concrete syntax(es), and the semantics, which turns into practical issues such as modifying editors, interpreters and compilers (or model transformations).

Some languages support self-extension. This means that the language contains abstractions to define new things (word used intentionally) that look to the user like a new language.

Examples include internal DSLs in Scala as well as UML profiles. The approach has the following advantages:

- since the new "languages" are built with the means of the host language, no additional (or specialized) meta tooling is necessary;
- the host languages are in some sense forward compatible because they allow users to build new "languages" without a change to the actual language definition of the host language. The forward compatibility is lost if the host language changes its means for defining new user-defined languages: languages defined with a newer version of the host language cannot be used with the old host languages. The various versions of Scala have this problem;
- also, the existing tools (IDEs, UML tools) can be used to work with these new, user-defined languages.

The approach of self-extension also has a number of drawbacks:

- In most cases the type system cannot be explicitly adapted to the user-defined language. This is most apparent in error messages which often report problems in terms of the underlying (meta-programming) implementation. C++ template meta programming and its infamous error messages come to mind.
- Also, the IDE usually is not explicitly aware of the user-defined language: debugging, refactoring and things like syntax coloring or code completion are not adapted (or require manual, specialized adaptations as in MagicDraw's custom editors).
- Finally, two extensions can collide – even if they can syntactically match, semantic clashes are common, and not easy to spot. The challenge here is how to reason about the composition of independently developed extensions, when they present some overlap (either because they can refer to the same elements, or because their semantics overlap).

The alternative to self extension is explicitly creating a new language from the existing one.

From the engineering point of view, a difficult problem is how modular this extension can be, for all the aspects of the language: concrete syntax, abstract syntax, static semantics, semantics, including interpreters or compilers.

At the concrete syntax level, the current state of the art with tools such as GMF or Xtext makes it extremely difficult to have this kind of modular extensions.

Conversely, at the meta-model, adding elements can be realized using some form of static introduction (i.e., considering meta-model classes as *open classes*). When the tool used to implement the meta-model does not natively support the required modular extension (e.g.; EMF based which is implemented in Java) however that's not so easy. Of course one can always copy the original meta-model MM1 into meta-model MM2, and manually add the extension, but then the fact that MM2 is an extension of MM1 is lost, so it is not going to be considered here. One possible technical solution is to work at the JVM level, using, e.g., AspectJ or Scala to weave the extension into the original metamodel. Kermeta is one example of compiling language parts into Scala to keep a good modularization for extensions of meta-models.

A second dimension of the modular extension problem is to make sure that everything that was written for MM1 is still working for its extension MM2. Here the notion of model typing, introduced in [32], is useful: if the extension MM2 is a subtype of MM1, that reuse of model transformations comes for free.

A model oriented typing system is the set of rules for deciding if substitutability between MM1 and MM2 is possible. When meta-models are defined in an object-oriented way (e.g., in EMF), it is clear that a model oriented typing system must somehow build on object-oriented typing systems. Substitutability is supported through subtyping in object-oriented languages. However, object subtyping does not handle type group specialization (i.e., the possibility to specialize relations between several objects and thus groups of types, see [7]). Thus, we need an extended definition of object type matching, as initially introduced by [4], and used by [13,32] to define a model type matching as a kind of subgraph isomorphism which takes into account the MOF specificities (e.g., inherited properties and operations).

With this particular form of extension where MM2 is a subtype of MM1, we can readily and safely reuse for MM2 models all the model manipulation operations (including model transformations) that have been defined for MM1. Still this subtyping is only structural. That can easily be extended to static semantics by considering OCL constraints as class invariants at the meta-modeling level: that's the idea of design by contract applied at the meta-model level. In practice however, making sure that a constraint added in the extension MM2 does not contradict an existing constraint of MM1 might need theorem proving for OCL, which is still a challenge despite many recent works, including those attempting to translate EMF+OCL to Alloy [1].

Even more challenging is to ensure behavioral subtyping, that is, the fact that the operational semantics of MM2 is a refinement of MM1's. Beyond toy languages, this is of course still an open challenge, but that must be solved for globalizing DSLs.

5.4 Externally Defined Correspondences (with Associated Constraints and Consistency Checks)

One of the problems of dealing with independent DSLs is ensuring that the prodels produced with these languages provide a *coherent* description of the target system. In the case of independent languages, the solution for relating them is by establishing a set of *correspondences* between them (see Fig. 1). Reasons for independent languages include:

– they may have been independently developed;
– they may have incompatible semantics;
– they need to be kept detached to allow the separation of concerns required to avoid complexity, or
– they may live in different tools.

   Correspondences do not form part of any one of the DSLs, but provide statements that relate the various different views—expressing their semantic relationships. Correspondences are needed to determine how the independent languages (and their associated models) fit together, and how they need to be related. They also enable checking the consistency of the descriptions provided by separate models, and permit reasoning about them.

   There is a fundamental difference between correspondences and references. In a reference from a language (or a prodel) to another, the first one is aware of the other. However, correspondences are "superimposed" (overlaid) on the language elements, or on the prodels, by an external designer, who establishes the relationships between them. These relationships are dependent on how we want to compose the languages, and both the languages and the prodels are completely unaware of them.

   Correspondences also have other important uses. For example, since they identify the related elements in a multi-viewpoint specification, they can help to identify the elements that would be affected by a change (also known as tracing, for example to requirements [16]). Thus, they can be useful in performing some kind of what-if or impact analysis on the views. Similarly, the constraints associated with the correspondence rules can be used to maintain consistency in the viewpoint specifications. Consider, for example, a consistent set of models related by a set of correspondences. If we make a change in one of the models, in many situations it is possible to automatically propagate that change through the correspondences, thereby changing the other models so that the consistency is restored. In this context, correspondences act as the "binds" that link together the related elements, enabling the propagation of the changes to maintain consistency [27].

   Correspondences need to be specified at two levels, depending on whether they relate metamodel or model elements. In the first case, correspondences determine the relationships that should exist between concepts of the two DSLs to be combined. For example, if we are combining class diagrams with statecharts, a correspondence between the two language metamodels can specify that every UML class should be related to one or more statecharts (the ones that define the behavior of the instances of that class). But then, instances of such correspondences (called *correspondence links*) should be specified at the model level, identifying which are the individual statecharts that should be related to a particular class. Making an analogy with programming languages, you need to define first how the grammars of the two languages can be related, and then how two individual programs are related using such relations [34].

Most multi-viewpoint platforms, frameworks and languages assume that correspondences between viewpoints are trivially based on name equality between correspondent elements, and implicitly defined. Or, since the viewpoint languages are developed together, they may contain explicit references to *"tie together"* the viewpoints.

In fact, most proposals and tools for viewpoint modeling take a simplistic approach to matching based on names: if the same name appears in two views, they are assumed to represent two aspects of the same object. However, if the models are to be developed by separate teams, it is not safe to assume they share a single namespace, or that name assignments are unique, unless they share a common frame of reference (a well-defined real-world system, see Sect. 3.3). It is also often the case that the correspondences are not simply one-to-one; the relationships between elements will generally be more complex [19,27]. In fact, in many situations establishing correspondences becomes a very complex task, impossible to automate [20]. For example, when the correspondences relate complex structures without an obvious mapping between them, or when the related elements are of different nature. Similarly, establishing correspondences between non-structural elements such as constraints or pieces of behavior is not trivial, either.

Existing proposals for expressing correspondences use different alternatives, from OCL constraints to UML abstraction dependencies (in the case of UML-based specifications). In the more general case, model weaving techniques are used for relating the elements of different models, or even model transformation languages such as QVT [27].

In general there are basically two approaches to model correspondences between the views of a system: extensional and intensional [27].

Extensional approaches model correspondences between the particular elements of the views, similarly to what is done for 2D representation of 3D figures. However, in large systems the number of correspondences hinders their proper definition, management and maintenance: the system designer cannot deal with (or even properly define and visualize) thousands of correspondences [20].

Intensional approaches define correspondences as relations between types of model elements, using predicates, formulae, or constraints. However, this approach may hinder the understandability and usability of the specifications produced: for typical users of the specification, correspondences are easier to use, visualize and understand when they are drawn as relationships between individual elements in the views, instead of being expressed as formulae. Intensional approaches work very well, for instance, when every object of a certain type in a given view is related to another object in another view (i.e., when relations can be defined at the *type* level). However, there are cases in which correspondences need to be established between particular objects of a specification (as it happens when the user defines the specific objects in one view that should be related to others in another view). The problem is that at the type level it is not that simple and elegant to determine which particular objects should be related.

In addition to languages, models and correspondences, we also need to impose some further constraints that establish valid *well-formed rules* between all the elements involved in the multi-view specification. These rules permit declaring required correspondences between the elements, imposing constraints on how the correspondences are established and how the elements are related. In other words, correspondence rules express constraints that must be enforced for the set of elements from the two viewpoints being linked, and for the set of correspondences themselves.

Correspondence rules can also serve to provide information about the kind of relationship that links the elements; such as "uses", "implements", "replicates", etc. These kinds of relationship are not predetermined, but are normally defined by the system designers. This definition must include their semantics, indicating what they are to mean in this system specification.

Open Challenges. The complexity involved in the specification and analysis of systems using separate languages and correspondences between them has revealed a whole set of new challenges that need to be addressed, some in the short term, some in a further future.

Correctness of Specification of Correspondences. Specifying correspondences is a complex task. In the first place, it is error-prone and subject to mistakes. How to check that all necessary correspondences have been specified between the languages first, and then between the models? (*completeness*). How to ensure that the correspondences between the views define one system, and that this system is precisely the one we have in mind, or the one that we have to represent? (*consistency*).

Nowadays consistency is proved by finding the existence of a system (or a model of it) that fulfills the specification. Although this may be a solution from a theoretical point of view, it is unrealistic in practice—especially, with the current tools that we have now.

And even if we manage to build a unified model using the views and the correspondences that bind them, such a model, once constructed, will show the problems of scale and complexity that led us to opt for viewpoints in the first place. The benefits, however, is that this model will not be for human consumption, but for tools to run checks and analyze the behavior of the system we have specified.

Usability of Specification of Correspondences. Usability is one of the limitations of most current modeling tools when they have to deal with large models. Writing large systems specifications becomes a tedious and cumbersome task. This is especially relevant in the case of the specification of correspondences, given that the number of correspondences is normally very large and the related elements need to be selected individually for each correspondence. Tools can be a great help in such a situation, and research is much needed for counting on tools that allow specifying correspondences in a usable and maintainable manner.

One example is provided by the annotation facilities of MPS, that permit adding information to the elements of one model, referencing related elements in another (as used in mbeddr requirements tracing). This mechanism is useful for specifying correspondences in a quick and user-friendly way. Then, from the annotated model it could be possible to extract the information about the correspondences themelves, annotate the counterpart model accordingly, etc. For example, mbeddr supports an assessment that reports all requirements and the program nodes that trace to it in one compact list [35].

As part of this, relating intensional and extensional correspondences need to be supported. Usually intensional correspondences are defined as relations between types of model elements, and this is done only once for every viewpoint modeling framework. However, there are situations in which the user wants to start the process by specifying correspondences in an extensional way. The question here is how to transform these extensional specifications into intensional ones (and vice-versa).

Methods and Tools to Specify the Correspondences. In summary, we need engineering methods for dealing with multi-viewpoint specifications that incorporate correspondences. How to specify, derive, implement, and maintain correspondences between viewpoints in a systematic, measurable and predictable manner?

What Happens with the Semantics? In general, combining the semantics of the languages related by correspondences is not a trivial task and deserves its own line of research. When composing languages, we need to consider the semantics of the individual languages and the semantics of the composition as such.

In a unification context, where there exists a unified model that integrates all views (hopefully, built by tools) the semantics of the individual DSLs and the unified language are preserved, and the (projection of the) results of the analysis conducted in the unified model are valid in the views. Hence, the unified model provides a common semantic platform compatible with the semantics of the views [3].

A major challenge is how tools can derive such a unified model from the viewpoint specifications, and from the correspondences between them. In this respect, there is presumably a scale of compatibility of semantics of languages under composition which makes composition easier or harder. The closer the semantic domain of the two languages, the easier the unification will be. One example of "easy" composition of semantics happens when we combine class diagrams and state machines. An example of a hard composition (if possible at all) happens when trying to combine the continuous time semantics of MATLAB or Simulink, with the discrete semantics of UML state machines.

Even when the semantics of the two languages are formally and explicitly stated, still the question arises whether they are "fit" for composition, not to mention when the semantics are not explicitly stated, as is normally the case. In this sense, the unified model can be very useful for providing a semantics for the separate models, in this common environment. Such semantics can be considered "the interpretation of those models" in the common semantic domain, and that precisely corresponds to the semantic domain of the system under study. The big challenge, here, is again the construction of such a unified model, and the development of the relationships between that model and the views [3,34].

5.5   All in One Tool vs. Different Tools

Globalization of DSLs is about integrating disparate prodeling languages and their tools in order to avoid semantic "surprises" (i.e., unexpected interactions on the model or physical levels). This integration includes several aspects, the most important being semantics: without a clear definition of what the integration of two languages means, there is not much point in integrating them. So semantic integration is obligatory and it may be defined in more or less strict ways based on a common frame of reference (see Sect. 3.3). Other aspects that are optional include syntactic integration (using the different languages in the same editor) and also tool integration (using one tool to manipulate models expressed in several languages).

The globalization of DSLs starts out with the premise that the languages continue to be used in their established tools so these tools can be reused. There are many arguments for this perspective:

- the tools are mature and have proven themselves to be useful to solve real-world problems in the domain,
- the tools themselves are stable (or at least the problems are well-known and can be worked around),
- the tools are established, so there is a lot of experience in the industry, the additional training effort is limited.

However, when trying to integrate a number of such tools, one runs into a number of problems, most of them related to the fact that many of these tools have not been designed to be open and integrable:

- the tools may not allow easy access to its data,
- the meta meta models of to-be-integrated tools may be incompatible [17],
- the scripting APIs may be limited so building exporters and importers is hard.

In addition, as long as the various languages continue to reside in separate tools, syntactic integration is impossible. Also, realtime collaboration (an update in one model is immediately visible in another) is hard(er) to achieve. So by definition, the integration of the languages is less "tight". In practice these problems can often be so daunting that we never get to the point of tackling the essential complexities involved in integrating the semantics; the integration project is canceled, DSL globalization does not happen.

An alternative approach for globalization is to re-implement established languages on a tool platform that is built for language integration and multi-concern modeling. Language workbenches such as MetaEdit+, Spoofax or MPS are built for this purpose. Below we list the advantages of this approach:

- All languages are based on the same meta meta model so referencing from one to the other is simple.
- Most language workbenches also support syntactic integration (embedding, extension).
- Cross-cutting concerns (such as requirements tracing, PLE variability or documentation) can be handled consistently throughout all the languages.
- The IDE experience for users is consistent, because all languages live in the same IDE.
- Language workbenches are built to be extended, so additional views, windows or utilities can be integrated easily.

Of course the price one pays is that the advantages of an existing, established, stable tool go away. Whether this is a problem may depend on the following considerations:

- Many organizations use only a small subset of an established tool. Rebuilding this subset of the required functionality/language may be feasible. If an existing tool is used fully, reimplementation based on a language workbench is less feasible.[3]
- The efforts for building languages with language workbenches are lower than most people expect, because language workbenches are built for this purpose.
- Essentially, the only remaining real challenge is the semantic integration.
- The essential complexity involved in semantic integration has to be solved in any case, though.

The decision between using established tools and integrating those vs. rebuilding the languages on top of a language workbench is not black and white. For example, one can build a core of closely collaborating languages on a language workbench, while still referencing outside model elements for less closely integrated concerns. Similarly, the various concerns relevant for a software

---

[3] In practice the decision is not so black-and-white but pragmatic: use e.g., modeling tool for the parts it work but yet provide integration for programming tools. (e.g., Visual Studio and Eclipse plug-ins in MetaEdit+). It is also questionable if there will even be such a platform that would be one for all users. For example today while Visual Studio (or Eclipse) are used for programming and some modeling tasks we can't expect that e.g., interaction specialists, safety engineers, requirements engineers etc. would use IDE style tool.

system (architecture, components, algorithms, implementation) can be done in a language workbench and the connections to systems-engineering level artifacts or requirements can be done as external references.

5.6   Process Aspects: Maybe We Should Stick with the Same Tool

We always take it for granted that we have to deal with different versions of tools or different tools. Maybe one alternative is to involve management to *force* everybody into the same tool. This is the approach followed, e.g., by UML, which tries to integrate all aspects into one modeling language, which can be supported by one single tool. Although the goal is laudable, this is normally unfeasible because no one single tool offers all functionality required in a project. Other tools try to integrate different languages and other tools into one single environment. But then we hit the problems mentioned above. The quest for a single tool that successfully satisfies the particular requirements of a company, either globally or within a set of projects is still an open line of research.

5.7   Tool/IDE Integration (Without Language Integration)

The actual integration of different languages can be either done on the syntactical level (language embedding) or by references. The references can point to concrete elements of other prodels or to some commonly known elements in the domain. As these references are usually just references by name there is often no need for changes on the syntactical level of the integrated languages. So in this case the languages can be developed completely independent even with different language workbenches and also used without knowing of each other in one or different IDEs.

However, as already stated earlier there is always a semantic integration behind using different languages for describing one system. Once the prodels should be validated for consistency with other prodels, simulated together, or transformed to the system level some kind of integration is needed. In case different IDEs are used to develop the prodels, the corresponding import/export mechanism to a common format or metamodel could be used. In this way the prodels could be even validated or simulated in an additional tool. However, just an export is not enough as error messages or the result of the simulation should be reported to the prodeler on the level of the involved prodels itself.

Another approach is to provide a common source of connecting elements and by making these accessible within the IDEs. In each IDE the prodels can then reference to these elements allowing to at least validate these references. The latest and also weakest point of integration is on the system level, which means that the prodels are transformed to code separately from each other in a way that the resulting system code is integrated. This approach only requires an agreement on interfaces on the system level for the transformation but has the drawback that inconsistencies cannot be automatically identified on the prodel level.

5.8   Interactivity: Realtime Sync, File Exchange, Shared DB

The least interactive (i.e., slowest) form of interaction is file-based. Tool T1 uses the persisted model file created by T2 as a means of learning about (and then, referencing or checking against) the model elements available. To make new model elements available, T2 must update (or re-export) the file. This requires explicit coordination between the (users of the) two tools. On the plus side, this approach provides a degree of isolation of T1 from the changes made in T2: It is the choice of the user of T1 to work against an updated file. This approach works very well with file-based CVS.

A more immediate form of collaboration is T1 directly calling into T2 through some kind of service or API. Interaction is potentially immediate. This may be good or bad; no isolation of model M1 is provided for user U1 if and when user U2 changes model M2 at the same time. Also, T2 actually has to be running so T1 can call into T2. This has consequences with respect to resources and licenses. A model bus (such as Toolbus [2]) is a generalized version of this approach.

The most realtime integration is for the various models M1 and M2 to work on top of the same repository. The repository can be file based (for example, a set of EMF files deployed in the same Eclipse instance) or an actual database (as in MetaEdit+). Changes made in M2 are directly visible to M1. Some form of explicit transaction control is useful to isolate the users from each other (for example, as provided by MetaEdit+). A database-based system has the drawback that it does not easily integrate with existing, file-based version control systems.

For the ideal language integration the versioning should be on the level of the language (aka domain it specifies). For example if a model is about insurance product the version should be a insurance product but not a number of files that specify it. In other words: domain sets the scope for versioning (not file system).

For integration, a tool may then put that (domain) like insurance product into a file for CVS, or version the whole repository, as today a hard disk is not a scarce resource anymore.

5.9   Collaborative Modeling

In terms of language and tool integration this section has focused on one developer at a time whereas at least in modeling space (and perhaps in programming space in future too) several persons can collaboratively work using different languages to specify the system (a bit like we creating the first version of this document in Google docs). So, collaboration on language and tool usage is something that cannot be ignored. Besides, it would also help to address some of the scalability issues mentioned before in the section, like that tools (storing models in file) don't scale to larger models (and teams). In several modeling tools it is common that multiple persons work collaboratively together (without having to diff and to merge models constantly) but that is not the case (at least not in practice) with programming tools currently. There is plenty of work to be done in this area, both at the research and development sides.

6   Language Variants (i.e., Parallel Globalization)

6.1   Dialects vs. Related Languages

As defined in Sect. 3.2, language variants are different languages used in parallel for similar purposes within the same domain, and thus typically sharing a common semantic domain.

When the variants V_i have a common ancestor A, V_i being dialects of A, it can be seen as a special case of language extensions as discussed above: V_i are extensions of A. There are cases however where the variants V_i do not have a common ancestor, but still share similars concepts giving them related forms. This is well known in biology evolution: for example sharks and dolphins somehow look alike (common points and variations), but they do not have (close) common ancestors. In the case of languages, let's take for example MOF, the class diagram of UML, and the structural subset of Java. All of them share the abstract concepts of classes, attributes, methods, inheritance, but they do not have a common concrete ancestor playing the role of a supertype of these languages. Sen et al. [30] provide and interesting approach to still be able to reuse model transformations (e.g., a refactoring such as the *pull-up method*) in that case: they propose to use the Adapter Pattern at the meta-model level, using in practice the Kermeta language to weave the adaptation code into the meta-models to make them look like having a common ancestor. Of course an interesting challenge is to see whether this approach scales for more complex cases.

6.2   Variability Management

Variability management is a mechanism for explicitly representing the commonalities and differences among a family of products that has been developed by the Software Product Line Engineering community over the last decades.

A family of products is defined as a set of software applications that have similar purposes and that share some functionality but that is specialized in a particular type of users or situation. The idea is to effectively reuse the implementation of such common functionality and having a repository of "common assets" that implement product features. The process of creating a product by using the family of products is called product derivation. To do so, it is necessary to select the desired product features and to offer a mechanism of composition for integrating the assets corresponding to each feature.

Variability management and the ideas behind SPLE in general, can be applied in the context of software languages for increasing reusability and then increasing the productivity of software language engineers. In this context, a family of products actually is a family of languages where there are some commonalities and some differences.

6.3   Challenges in Languages Variability Management

Alignment with the Modularization Approach. It is worth noting that modularization is a prerequisite for addressing variability management. In fact, at the implementation level software modularization and variability management are strongly linked. Each concrete feature expressed in the variability model must correspond to a software component in the architecture so that a given configuration can be derived in a concrete functional product. In the case of software languages each feature should be mapped to one (or more) language units that offers the corresponding services. Moreover, in [13] van der Linden et al. present a set of three variability realization techniques at the level of the software modularization schema. Those techniques can be viewed as a set of requirements in terms of modularization and composition of the architecture and they are quite related with the concepts of extension, substitutability and adaptation, some of them discussed in the previous section. How to conjugate all those concepts for effectively define an approach that allows the construction of families of software languages?

Multi-stage Orthogonal Variability Modeling. Typically, a software language specification is intended to define the abstract syntax, the concrete syntax and the semantics of a language. As a result, language units have to contribute to each of those dimensions. In other words, each language unit specification includes a partial definition of the abstract syntax, the concrete syntax, and the semantics. The whole language specification is obtained by putting all the language units together. In [8] the authors observed that there exists some variability between each of those dimensions. Thereby, one language construct (i.e., a concept in the abstract syntax) may be represented in several ways (i.e., several possible concrete syntaxes) and/or may have different meanings (several possible semantics). This analysis remains the same for both the whole language specification and each segment defined in language units. Consequently, we have at least three different dimensions of variability each of them regarding one field of the tuple:

Abstract syntax variability or *functional variability*: This variability refers to the capability of selecting the desired language constructs for a particular product as long as the dependencies are respected. Consider for example a family of languages for state machines where concepts such as timed transitions, composite states, or history pseudo-states are optional and are only included if the user of the language needs them. This variability dimension is quite similar to the classical concept of functional variability of SPLE where each feature represents a piece of functionality that may be or not included depending on the specific requirements of a user.

Concrete syntax variability or *representation variability*: This variability refers to the capability of offering different representations for the same concept. Consider for example a language for state machines that can have textual or graphical representations.

Semantics variability or *interpretation variability*: This variability refers to capability of offering the different interpretations to the same concept. Consider for example the semantics differences that exist between state machines languages explored in [4]. In that work, we can see how, for example, the priorities between conflicting transitions in a state machine are resolved with different criteria. If we are able to manage such variability, the reuse opportunities are drastically increased since we are able to reuse the entire language infrastructure (e.g., editors, abstract syntax trees) for the implementation of different languages that are interpreted according to the needs of specific users.

Note that both representation variability and interpretation variability depend on the functional variability. It makes no sense to select a representation (or interpretation) for a language construct that has not been included as part of the language product. In other words, the configuration of representation and interpretation must be performed only for the construct selected in the functional variability resolution.

7   Language Evolution, Refactoring, Retirement (i.e., Sequential Globalization)

As any other software artifacts, DSLs and the prodels written in them are subject to evolution: new requirements force the addition or modification of some language features; parts of the language are restructured to accommodate improvements and to permit optimizations; some features become deprecated as others appear. Globalized ecosystems, as any other ecosystem, should take into account the life cycle and evolution of their elements.

Language version concerns the evolution of one language *over time*. Usually only one version of a language is used in a project at a moment in time. This is in contrast with the variants discussed above, which are indeed different languages (although they are for the same purpose and within the same domain), used *at the same time* in a project.

In general, language versions can be produced in different ways, some of which have been discussed above. For example, language extensions can be considered as (backwards compatible) language versions that incorporate new features, producing a new version of an existing language in an ordered, systematic and predictable way. Other changes to the language can produce new versions in a less structured and controlled manner, causing, e.g., backwards incompatibility issues.

This issue also brings along the problem of the co-evolution of the software ecosystem artifacts [28]. For example, model and metamodel co-evolution: it happens when a metamodel changes and the models are no longer conformant to the new metamodel. Should we leave them as they are? Should we make them evolve? And if we decide to make them evolve, is it possible? Is it automatable?

Other interesting co-evolution problem happens a model transformation needs to change when any of the metamodels it handles changes [29]. There is also the traditional problem of instance migration in databases when an schema changes[4].

Forward compatibility needs also be considered, since it starts to be commonplace in extensible languages (such as, e.g., Scala). This kind of compatibility is lost if the host language changes how new user-defined (guest) languages are defined, hindering its use with previously defined guest languages. Forward compatibility is much harder to achieve than backward compatibility because forward-compatible languages need to deal with unknown future features.

Finally, languages also retire, and the legacy prodels they leave behind must be either maintained or modernized. These are decisions that involve not only technical considerations but also (and overall) economical and social aspects.

In this context, Model Transformations have an essential role to play. A model transformation provides the operationalization of the specification of the relation between two or more languages. Thus, they can be used not only to specify the relationship between two versions of a language, but also to help migrating the corresponding artifacts and prodels, in an automated manner.

References

1. Anastasakis, K., Bordbar, B., Georg, G., Ray, I.: On challenges of model transformation from UML to alloy. Softw. Syst. Model. **9**(1), 69–86 (2010)
2. Bergstra, J.A., Klint, P.: The ToolBus coordination architecture. In: Hankin, C., Ciancarini, P. (eds.) COORDINATION 1996. LNCS, vol. 1061, pp. 75–88. Springer, Heidelberg (1996)
3. Bowman, H., Steen, M., Boiten, E.A., Derrick, J.: A formal framework for viewpoint consistency. Formal Methods Syst. Des. **21**(2), 111–166 (2002)
4. Bruce, K.B., Schuett, A., van Gent, R., Fiech, A.: Polytoil: a type-safe polymorphic object-oriented language. ACM Trans. Program. Lang. Syst. **25**(2), 225–290 (2003)
5. Dinkelaker, T., Eichberg, M., Mezini, M.: An architecture for composing embedded domain-specific languages. In: Jézéquel, J.-M., Südholt, M. (eds.) Proceedings of the 9th International Conference on Aspect-Oriented Software Development, AOSD 2010, pp. 49–60. ACM, Rennes, Saint-Malo, 15–19 March 2010
6. Erdweg, S., Giarrusso, P.G., Rendel, T.: Language composition untangled. In: Sloane, A., Andova, S. (eds.) International Workshop on Language Descriptions, Tools, and Applications, LDTA 2012, p. 7. ACM, Tallinn, 31 March–1 April 2012
7. Ernst, E.: Family polymorphism. In: Lindskov Knudsen, J. (ed.) ECOOP 2001. LNCS, vol. 2072, pp. 303–326. Springer, Heidelberg (2001)
8. Erwig, M., Walkingshaw, E.: Semantics first! - rethinking the language design. In: Sloane, A., Aßmann, U. (eds.) SLE 2011. LNCS, vol. 6940, pp. 243–262. Springer, Heidelberg (2012)
9. Fowler, M.: Language workbenches: the killer-app for domain specific languages? (2005)
10. Fritzsche, M., Johannes, J., Aßmann, U., Mitschke, S., Gilani, W., Spence, I., Brown, J., Kilpatrick, P.: Systematic usage of embedded modelling languages in automated model transformation chains. In: Gašević, D., Lämmel, R., Van Wyk, E. (eds.) SLE 2008. LNCS, vol. 5452, pp. 134–150. Springer, Heidelberg (2009)

---

[4] http://martinfowler.com/articles/evodb.html.

11. Ghosh, D.: Dsl for the uninitiated. Queue **9**(6), 10:10–10:21 (2011)
12. Gill, A.: Domain-specific languages and code synthesis using haskell. Queue **12**(4), 30:30–30:43 (2014)
13. Guy, C., Combemale, B., Derrien, S., Steel, J.R.H., Jézéquel, J.-M.: On model subtyping. In: Vallecillo, A., Tolvanen, J.-P., Kindler, E., Störrle, H., Kolovos, D. (eds.) ECMFA 2012. LNCS, vol. 7349, pp. 400–415. Springer, Heidelberg (2012)
14. Hudak, P.: Modular domain specific languages and tools. In: Devanbu, P., Poulin, J., (eds.) Proceeding of the 5th International Conference on Software Reuse (ICSR 1998), pp. 134–142. IEEE (1998)
15. Hudak, P.: Building domain-specific embedded languages. ACM Comput. Surv. **28**(4es), 196 (1996)
16. Jarke, M.: Requirements tracing. Commun. ACM **41**(12), 32–36 (1998)
17. Kern, H., Stefan, F., Dimitrieski, V., Celikovic, M.: Mapping-based exchange of models between meta-modeling tools. In: Proceedings of the DSM Forum at SPLASH 2014, ACM DL (2014). http://www.dsmforum.org/events/DSM14/Papers/Kern.pdf
18. Kosar, T., López, P.E.M., Barrientos, P.A., Mernik, M.: A preliminary study on various implementation approaches of domain-specific language. Inf. Softw. Technol. **50**(5), 390–405 (2008)
19. Linington, P.: Black cats and coloured birds what do viewpoint correspondences do? In: Proceedings of WODPEC 2007, Maryland, USA, October 2007
20. Linington, P.F., Milosevic, Z., Tanaka, A., Vallecillo, A.: Building Enterprise Systems with ODP - An Introduction to Open Distributed Processing. Chapman and Hal/CRC innovations in software engineering and software development. CRC Press, Boca Raton (2011)
21. Mernik, M.: An object-oriented approach to language compositions for software language engineering. J. Syst. Softw. **86**(9), 2451–2464 (2013)
22. Mernik, M., Heering, J., Sloane, A.M.: When and how to develop domain-specific languages. ACM Comput. Surv. **37**(4), 316–344 (2005)
23. Oracle.: Pro*c/c++ programmer's guide 10g release 2 (10.2) (2005)
24. Oracle.: Oracle database sqlj developer's guide and reference 11g release 1 (11.1) (2007)
25. Oracle.: The java^{TM} tutorials: Jdbc(tm) database access (2014)
26. Oracle.: Oracle database sql language reference 11g release 2 (11.2) (2014)
27. Romero, J.R., Jaén, J.I., Vallecillo, A.: Realizing correspondences in multi-viewpoint specifications. In: Proceedings of EDOC 2009, pp. 163–172. IEEE Computer Society, Auckland, September 2009
28. Di Ruscio, D., Iovino, L., Pierantonio, A.: Coupled evolution in model-driven engineering. IEEE Softw. **29**(6), 78–84 (2012)
29. Di Ruscio, D., Iovino, L., Pierantonio, A.: A methodological approach for the coupled evolution of metamodels and ATL transformations. In: Duddy, K., Kappel, G. (eds.) ICMB 2013. LNCS, vol. 7909, pp. 60–75. Springer, Heidelberg (2013)
30. Sen, S., Moha, N., Mahé, V., Barais, O., Baudry, B., Jézéquel, J.-M.: Reusable model transformations. Softw. Syst. Model. **11**(1), 111–125 (2012)
31. Spinellis, D.: Notable design patterns for domain-specific languages. J. Syst. Softw. **56**(1), 91–99 (2001)
32. Steel, J., Jézéquel, J.-M.: On model typing. Softw. Syst. Model. **6**(4), 401–413 (2007)
33. Sun, Y., Demirezen, Z., Mernik, M., Gray, J., Bryant, B.: Is my DSL a modeling or programming language? In: Lawall, J., Réveillère, L. (eds.) Domain-Specific Program Development, p. 4, Nashville, United States (2008)

34. Vallecillo, A.: On the combination of domain specific modeling languages. In: Kühne, T., Selic, B., Gervais, M.-P., Terrier, F. (eds.) ECMFA 2010. LNCS, vol. 6138, pp. 305–320. Springer, Heidelberg (2010)
35. Voelter, M., Ratiu, D., Tomassetti, F.: Requirements as first-class citizens: integrating requirements closely with implementation artifacts. In: ACESMB@MoDELS (2013)

Domain Globalization: Using Languages to Support Technical and Social Coordination

Julien Deantoni[1], Cédric Brun[2(✉)], Benoit Caillaud[3], Robert B. France[4], Gabor Karsai[5], Oscar Nierstrasz[6], and Eugene Syriani[7]

[1] University of Nice-Sophia-Antipolis, Nice, France
[2] Obeo, Carquefou, France
cedric.brun@obeo.fr
[3] INRIA, Rennes, France
[4] University of Colorado, Boulder, CO, USA
[5] Vanderbilt University, Nashville, TN, USA
[6] University of Bern, Bern, Switzerland
[7] University of Montreal, Montreal, Canada

Abstract. When a project is realized in a globalized environment, multiple stakeholders from different organizations work on the same system. Depending on the stakeholders and their organizations, various (possibly overlapping) concerns are raised in the development of the system. In this context a Domain Specific Language (DSL) supports the work of a group of stakeholders who are responsible for addressing a specific set of concerns. This chapter identifies the open challenges arising from the coordination of globalized domain-specific languages. We identify two types of coordination: technical coordination and social coordination. After presenting an overview of the current state of the art, we discuss first the open challenges arising from the composition of multiple DSLs, and then the open challenges associated to the collaboration in a globalized environment.

Keywords: Composition · Coordination · DSL · Globalization

1 Context

In this chapter we describe the issues associated with the coordination aspects of the globalizing languages challenge. Specifically, the focus is on how globalized domain-specific languages (DSLs) can be used on projects with multiple stakeholder groups, each focusing on a different engineering/development concern, to support analysis of system properties and coordination of work across the groups. The groups may span multiple organizations that temporarily need to collaborate on a project, thus one needs to accommodate different collaboration styles and engineering cultures, and manage differing trust and security procedures when it comes to sharing information. The language-based coordination mechanisms should take these into consideration.

© Springer International Publishing Switzerland 2015
B.H.C. Cheng et al. (Eds.): Globalizing Domain-Specific Languages, LNCS 9400, pp. 70–87, 2015.
DOI: 10.1007/978-3-319-26172-0_5

In this context, a DSL is a software or system language that is specifically built to support the work of a group of stakeholders that are responsible for addressing a specific set of concerns. It must therefore be supported by technologies that serve the particular purposes of the stakeholders. For example, a DSL's purpose may be to support static analysis of properties, provide a description of a system component, or it may be used to support simulation of some behavioral aspect. Based on purpose, a DSL may be declarative, executable, prescriptive or descriptive.

A distinguishing characteristic of a globalized framework of DSLs is its openness, that is, there is no restriction on the form of languages and supporting tools that can be added to the framework. Realizing the globalized DSL vision thus requires consideration of how new DSLs and their toolsets are incorporated into the language framework.

Two types of language-based coordination can be broadly identified: Technical and Social. Technical coordination is concerned with the mechanisms used to compose heterogeneous languages to support analysis of properties that require information captured in models expressed in different languages. Such analysis typically requires coordinated analysis of the models expressed in the different languages. Examples of two forms of analysis are consistency checking and compatibility checking. Checking consistency means to determine whether information spread across models expressed in different languages is not contradictory. This is easily understood when considering DSLs expressing logical or numerical constraints where checking consistency amounts to checking the satisfiability of the conjunction of the constraints. In system engineering, consistency usually applies to models belonging to the various viewpoints of the same component. Compatibility checking is concerned with determining whether two models can be composed in a particular environment, that is, two models are compatible if there is an environment in which two models can work together. The simplest instance of this concept is the type compatibility of components with input and output ports, where the output of one component should be a subtype of the input of the other components. Compatibility usually applies to models of several interacting components that form a system architecture.

To support technical coordination, correspondences between language elements should be defined at the syntactic level. Elements for identifying and describing such correspondences needs to be supported.

Language-based social coordination is concerned with how globalized DSLs can be used to support effective collaboration across stakeholder groups. Coordination of work through globalized software languages leads to social translucence, where relatively autonomous groups of stakeholders are made aware of activities performed by other groups. Groups can thus react accordingly to communicated information and in turn notify other groups of their reactions. These interactions can take place through the sending of notifications and feedback. Social coordination can also include support for managing resources across groups. To support social coordination the DSLs may have, for example, to be augmented with metadata about activities and resources associated with the DSL language elements.

2   State of Art

Multiple DSLs can be composed into a host environment at a variety of different levels. The coarsest level is that of *tool composition*, where tools supporting a domain modeling approach may be composed, but there is no language composition per se. With *model composition*, the underlying models can interact, but again there is no language composition. Finally, with *language composition*, individual DSLs may be integrated or coordinated, either at a syntactic level or at a deeper semantic level.

2.1   Tool Composition Frameworks

Tool composition frameworks provide a means for individual tools to interact with one another. "Tool" here can mean a model editing or model execution environment, but in practice they may include simpler tools like spreadsheets. The tools may be domain-specific or general-purpose, and tool composition frameworks facilitate tool interoperability. Several tool integration patterns have been developed and used in complex toolchains [5,10,29,31]. Tool chains may support collaborative work, either directly (when a multitude of developers is assisted by the framework, in real-time, synchronously), or indirectly (when the collaboration is more asynchronous).

Some tool integration frameworks are distributed (with tools running on different platforms), some are desktop-based, where the framework provides a unified visual interface to a suite of the integrated tools. For the latter **Eclipse**[1] is the most prevalent example. Commercial products are also available[2].

There also exist tool coordination frameworks whose goal is to orchestrate the execution/simulation driven by different tools so that data can be exchanged between them during the simulation. One of the best-known coordination framework is the functional mock-up interface [7].

2.2   Model Composition Frameworks

The purpose of model composition is to provide a consistent view of various models possibly expressed in different modeling languages for the purposes of analysis and synthesis. The challenge is that the domain, the syntax, and the semantics of modeling languages can be widely different, yet the composed model has to have a semantics on its own that is relevant for the task at hand. Broadly speaking, models can be composed either via a hierarchy or via side-by-side composition. In hierarchical composition models coming from one language are embedded in models expressed in another language, while in side-by-side composition models at the same level of abstraction are related, usually via their interfaces. Models can be static artifacts (*i.e.*, passive documents) or dynamic entities (*e.g.*, models embedded within a simulation engine). Hence, model integration can be

---

[1] http://en.wikipedia.org/wiki/Eclipse_Modeling_Framework.
[2] http://www.phoenix-int.com/software/phx-modelcenter.php.

static or dynamic, yielding either a composed (static) document or an active, integrated dynamic model executing on some platform. In all model integration frameworks, there is some common foundation to support integration. This could be syntactic, semantic, operational, or some mixture. By syntactic foundation we mean a concrete textual or visual notation that allows model integration; by semantic foundation we mean a common semantic domain, and by operational foundation we mean some software infrastructure that allows the inter-operation of models.

UML Profiles provide a mechanism for defining and composing domain-specific modeling languages in the overall UML framework. These are not new languages, but already defined UML constructs that are specialized through stereotyping. Stereotypes are special markers applied to specific UML model elements, which gain a specific semantics through this process. Profiles often specify model patterns (built from stereotyped model elements) that have domain-specific semantics. In this case the model integration platform is UML, and the integration is supported by the model integration operators of UML.

Coordination languages encompass both the formalisms and the mechanisms needed to achieve multiple parallel, possibly distributed computation. Their purpose is to coordinate a number of possibly heterogeneous executable models together, by interfacing with each of them in such a way that they can take advantage of parallel and distributed systems [25]. Examples of such languages are Linda [12] for data-driven coordination, or Esper[3] for event-driven coordination. These languages emphasize the benefits of having an explicit coordination model to reason about the coordination of multiple executable models.

The **CyPhy**[4] [47] modeling language was developed to facilitate model coordination for the design of complex cyber-physical systems, for instance vehicles. This model coordination language is built around a hierarchical component model where components have four categories of interfaces: parametric and properties (for setting and getting parametric values), signal interfaces (for causal interactions among electronic and software components), power interfaces (for acausal interactions among physical components with dynamics), and structural interfaces (for geometric 3D composition). CyPhy components contain references for high-fidelity domain-specific models stored in external modeling tools and model databases. CyPhy models are composed by connecting the strongly-typed component interfaces so that the composite allows a coordinated analysis of the entire system. Note that the analysis can cut across many different domain-specific models.

The **High-Level Architecture**[5] (HLA) (IEEE-1516) [34] is a run-time framework for coordinating heterogeneous distributed simulation engines, called federates. It provides a standard for facilitating interaction among simulations, including message formats and the synchronization of the logical clocks of the simulators. Each simulation preserves its own semantics for the model, but as

---

[3] http://www.espertech.com/esper/.

[4] http://cps-vo.org/group/avm/meta-overview.

[5] http://en.wikipedia.org/wiki/High-level_architecture_(simulation).

simulations advance in time, their clocks remain synchronized. The semantics of the federation (composed from the federates) is that of a large-scale dynamic system where each component has its own dynamics, yet the temporal progression of the individual engines is carefully regulated.

2.3 Language Composition Frameworks

Language integration frameworks enable the embedding of multiple DSLs into a host language. This integration is commonly at a *syntactic* level. The composition may also be done at a deeper *semantic* level either by integration or by coordination.

Syntactic Integration. Syntactic integration of domain-specific languages is commonly supported by so-called *language workbenches* [22], environments that define (1) a schema for an abstract syntax for a language (*i.e.*, a grammar), (2) one or more rich editing environments for the language, and (3) language semantics, typically either by direct interpretation or code generation. Language workbenches can be based on a variety of parsing technologies, such as generalized LR (GLR) parsing [48], generalized LL (GLL) parsing [43], term rewriting [23], parser combinators [24], or parsing expression grammars [9].

AToMPM[6] [46] is a framework for generating syntax-directed domain-specific modeling editors, performing in-place model transformation, and managing DSMs in a cloud-based web environment. Each DSL has one meta-model. However, a model can be built that links instances from different meta-models, therefore a model can conform to multiple meta-models. A DSL can be assigned multiple graphical concrete syntaxes.

AToMPM follows a view-based modeling approach. A user only interacts with a view of a model, specified in a dedicated concrete syntax, showing a sub-set of the underlying model. Changes in one view are automatically propagated to the model and to other overlapping views. Multiple users can collaboratively work on the same view. Concurrent conflicting changes are handled by manual inspection through a chatting system.

Helvetia[7] [40] is a PEG-based language workbench for adding DSLs to Smalltalk by source code transformation. The transformations are available to the entire language toolchain, so tools like the editor and the debugger can exploit them to accurately display the original embedded DSL source rather than just the generated host language code.

MetaEdit+[8] is a mature language workbench that supports graphical diagram, matrix and table representations for DSLs. Languages can be composed by integrating individual metamodels or by creating a metamodel that includes several integrated languages. A language definition is integrated combining abstract

---

[6] http://www-ens.iro.umontreal.ca/~syriani/atompm/atompm.htm.

[7] http://scg.unibe.ch/research/helvetia.

[8] http://www.metacase.com/.

syntax, static semantics, concrete syntax and transformations. MetaEdit+ supports collaborative language engineering allowing several persons to create DSLs at the same time as well as it supports collaborative modeling when using the DSLs. It is a commercial and supported environment that is used to create hundreds of DSLs.

TXL[9] [15] is a source code transformation language based on term rewriting. TXL can be used to transform embedded DSLs to a host language, much like Helvetia. **Spoofax**[10] [37] is a language workbench based on term rewriting. Spoofax offers a fine degree of control over the term rewriting traversal strategy.

MPS[11] is a platform enabling the definition and integration of DSLs through the use of language extensions and projectional editing. Rather than manipulating a program as a text, MPS stores a program as an abstract syntax tree (AST) and edits it directly. MPS enables embedding of a language into another while avoiding the problem of textual grammar ambiguity by not storing language code as text at all but storing the AST and reifying the notion of *Language Extension*: a set of concepts that refine those present in the base model with their own attributes and references.

The **Generic Modeling Environment** (**GME**) [36][12] is a metaprogrammable graphical modeling environment that enables the definition of graphical modeling languages through metamodels. Once defined, the metamodel can immediately be used in a domain-specific graphical model editor that enforces the use of concepts, integration operators, and well-formedness rules (*i.e.*, the structural semantics) of the domain-specific modeling language defined by the metamodel. The tool has its own meta-metamodel, and provides model access API-s, both on the meta- (*i.e.*, language-) level and the domain (*i.e.*, model-) level. Metamodels of languages are composable within the tool, allowing the integration of domain-specific modeling languages. The most recent development in GME (called WebGME[13]) provides a web-based collaborative graphical modeling environment with version control and support for distributed model editing.

Dictō [11] follows a lightweight approach to integrating architectural constraint checkers. Rather than integrating multiple DSLs, it offers a single, syntactical framework for expressing different kinds of architectural constraints, and allows tools for checking those constraints to be plugged into the Dictō framework.

Semantic Composition. When the system consists of different executable languages, it is of primary importance to understand what are the emerging behaviors (whether expected or not) of the global system. In such cases it is necessary to understand how the semantics of each language can be composed. The goal of the semantic composition is to enable simulation and/or verification activities on the global system according to (1) the semantics of each language

---

[9] http://www.txl.ca/.
[10] http://strategoxt.org/Spoofax/WebHome.
[11] http://www.jetbrains.com/mps/.
[12] http://www.isis.vanderbilt.edu/Projects/gme/.
[13] http://webgme.org/.

and (2) the behavior scattered in/specified by the heterogeneous models (*i.e.*, the models conforming to different languages). In consequence actual approaches for semantic composition are usually ensure that the coordination of the models conforming to these languages can be automatically obtained. There exist very different approaches to deal with this problem.

A first kind of approach, typified by **Formula**[14] [21] or **Modelyze**[15] [8], provides a formal environment where you can define, based on a specific form of the grammar, the domain-specific semantics of your language. This involves a translation of the domain-specific language into a representation suitable for formal anchoring in the targeted tool. In these approaches, the underlying semantics of these environment acts as a common semantic domain from which reasoning is possible. Based on a common representation of the semantics, it is then possible to specify how they are related. Such an approach provides very interesting formal verification capabilities, but a first drawback is the need for an arbitrarily complex transformation, which can make the semantics of the original model difficult to handle. This drawback is often pointed out in more classical approaches using translational semantics (*i.e.*, the translation of a semantic free language into a common formal representation). The other drawback relies on the existence of a common semantic background that must be expressive enough to be suitable for a wide variety of language while staying well founded for verification and validation activities.

A second kind of approach makes explicit the notion of a Model of Computation (MoC) [18,26,42]. In these approaches, a MoC specifies the causalities, timing and synchronization aspects of a language. First, making a MoC explicit enables fine tuning of the computational semantics, and usually offers simulation facilities. Second, it enables a clear specification of some semantic adaptations between different MoCs so that the semantics of heterogeneous models can be consistently coordinated. These approaches provide either the capacity to adapt to a domain-specific language (**Ptolemy** [18]) or **Modhel'X** [26]) or the capacity to drive formal refinement and reasoning on the system (**Forsyde** [42]), hence forcing the designer to choose between domain adequacy and analysis power.

A third kind of approach is based on the notion of meta-languages. It provides meta-languages for the specification of the domain-specific syntax (abstract and concrete) but also meta-languages for the specification of the semantics and its mapping to the syntax [14]. When using a meta-language like **Ecore** [45], you benefit from the associated generative techniques like the generation of a simple editor, its API, *etc.* In the same way, when using the meta-language for behavioral semantics specification, you can draw benefits from the automated generation of an interpreter and a explorer, making the models executable. The same advantage is obtained when using a meta-language for behavioral semantic composition, like BCOoL [49]. The main drawback of this approach comes from the meta-language for behavioral semantics specification, which is not suitable for an adequate specification of acausal models.

---

[14] http://research.microsoft.com/en-us/projects/formula/.
[15] https://github.com/david-broman/modelyze.

3 Open Challenges

The key challenge in the globalization of domain-specific languages is naturally how to compose multiple languages, both syntactically and semantically within a single software system. But there is another challenge related to collaboration in a globalized environment. It includes the management of the individual artifacts over time, environmental support for the viewpoints of multiple stakeholders, and scalable, persistent management of diverse models in a global environment.

We will survey each of these challenges and their associated research questions in turn.

3.1 Composition of Multiple DSLs

The composition of multiple DSLs for the construction of a single software system entails a number of fundamental questions. How are such languages composed syntactically and semantically? Can we view DSLs as components, and, if so, what are their interfaces? How can we determine if languages are semantically compatible, and how can we check if the models expressed in them are consistent? Finally, how can we integrate legacy tools tied to individual DSLs within a common integrated system?

How Do We Compose Languages? State of the art approaches have mainly focused on the syntactic integration of languages. They specify operators for *merging* the abstract syntaxes of different DSLs. A first challenge would be to identify and to classify the integration operators and their impact on the properties of the composed language [13,19]. Existing approaches seldom deal with the behavioral semantics of the integration. Beyond the syntactic composition, another challenge is therefore to extend the classification to cover the semantic aspects of languages.

In many language composition approaches, the composition operators are specified on languages but the integration (*i.e.*, the merging) itself is applied on models. They use the knowledge of the meta-language to specify the composition. Yet another challenge is to understand if it makes sense to adapt such an idea to the behavioral semantics of language. In this case a directly associated challenge would be to understand what kind of meta-languages can describe the behavioral semantics of one language. Then, during the behavioral composition of languages, does the composition integrate the behavioral semantics of the languages or is it used to coordinate the behaviors of models that conform the languages?

Can We View Languages as Components? If So, What Are their Interfaces? Component-Based Software Engineering was quite successful in abstracting pieces of code or binary behind interfaces. Interfaces can be used to coordinate multiple components without requiring any knowledge of the components' internal implementation. This idea has penetrated many domain-specific languages so that models can be seen as components equipped with interfaces to enable their coordination. The challenge now is to see the languages themselves as components, meaning that they can be equipped with purpose-specific interfaces. Beyond the agreement that an interface is an abstraction of the language, the exact nature of the interface is far from clear. For instance, if one sees a language as a specification of a set of models describable in this language, then an interface could offer a way to specify the subset of models supported by the purpose the interface relates to. However, it can also be the set of operators, together with a characterization of what it accepts from the language. It is not clear also if the interface of a language can be used for language integration or only for language coordination.

Many sub-questions arises from this challenge *e.g.*, does it make sense to provide some family of language interfaces according to some purpose at the model level [1,47]? Another research question is: in what language should a language's interface be specified? Should such a specification be reflexive at some point?

Does a Composed System Have a Unified Semantics? Semantic composition means that one can analyze the properties of the composition of a set of models expressed in several DSLs. This analysis can be manual, based on experts' knowledge, and possibly on a precise mathematical semantics of the composition, or it can be automated. If the analysis is to be automated, then the semantics of the composition of DSLs has to be implemented in some way. This can range from simple type-checking rules to the composition of heterogeneous behavior paradigms: for instance asynchronous processes coupled with time-triggered processes, or the coupling of discrete-time and continuous-time dynamical systems.

How can this be achieved in practice? At a first glance, a common semantic domain could be defined and implemented. Analysis would be performed using the methods and tools of this unified semantic domain. Unfortunately, unified semantic domains would become inconceivably complex when composing more than a few DSLs. Unified semantic domains would be very expressive, and not surprisingly, even the simplest analyses might turn out to be undecidable. The unified semantic domain approach certainly has practical value whenever the semantic domains to be unified are not too dissimilar.

Another approach is to avoid implementing a unified semantic domain, but rather to provide means to coordinate the different models (*e.g.*, by constructing on-the-fly combined heterogeneous behavior). This is best understood when the DSLs describe event-based discrete-time behavior, and each DSL comes with a transition system based operational semantics. In Gemoc Studio[16], behavior synchronization is achieved on-the-fly, without recourse to an explicit, unified semantic domain. In Ptolemy II[17], programs called directors are used not only to define models of computation, but also to define how low-level synchronization between heterogeneous components is achieved.

---

[16] http://gemoc.org/studio.
[17] http://ptolemy.eecs.berkeley.edu/ptolemyII/index.htm.

Composing models with dissimilar semantic domains is largely an open problem. There are even semantic domains in which composability is difficult to achieve. A striking example is that of stochastic systems: they are difficult to compose, unless drastic stochastic independence assumptions are made.

Challenges in DSL Semantic Composition. Semantic composition can be achieved using several *ad-hoc* techniques, depending on the semantics to be composed. Event-based operational semantics, often used for state machines or dataflow programs can easily be composed by synchronizing the step functions of their concrete semantics. The same principle applies to timed extensions of these formalisms, namely timed automata, and the network calculus. The subject is however still in its infancy and no clear methodology has been proposed to address the composition of arbitrary semantic domains. We review below several hard cases of semantic composition.

Composition of Discrete-Time and Continuous-Time Models. How can one co-simulate a system combining models with radically different semantics: discrete time dynamical systems on one hand, and continuous time dynamical systems on the other hand? The discrete time dynamics is often expressed in a data flow or automata based language, while the continuous dynamics results from a system of ordinary or algebraic differential equations (resp. ODEs and DAEs). Several techniques can be used to address this problem, depending on the overall system architecture and the assumptions that can be made on the overall system behaviour. These techniques range from simple asymmetric co-simulation methods, where time is handled by a unique numerical solver, to more involved techniques combining several numerical solvers. With the Functional Mock-up Interface[18], several models mixing continuous and discrete time dynamics can be co-simulated, with the restriction that the whole continuous-time dynamics is handled by a unique numerical solver. Proposals have been put forward to extend FMI, with for instance roll-back and step-size prediction mechanisms, to support a deterministic co-simulation with several variable step-size numerical solvers [17]. These techniques suffer from poor parallelism, and are difficult to implement on a distributed parallel architecture, making them unusable on large system models. Radically different techniques with good parallelism have been explored, but for limited classes of models. For example, Waveform Relaxation is a distributed simulation method for continuous-time dynamical systems, with superlinear convergence properties under mild Lipschitz smoothness assumptions [51]. An interesting challenge would be to extend Waveform Relaxation techniques to the hybrid systems case.

Composition of Acausal Models. A key challenge is the compositionality of acausal continuous time models. They are often expressed using algebraic differential equations (DAEs), where the data flow orientation of an incomplete

---

[18] https://www.fmi-standard.org.

model may depend on its environment. This makes the generation of simulation code from a component model a difficult problem. The reason is that the environment of a component is not known before this component instantiated in a closed model. This problem becomes even harder when considering hybrid systems with DAEs, found for example in the Modelica language[19]. The main reason is that both the dataflow orientation and the differentiation index may change dynamically, depending on the discrete state of the model. This has severe consequences on the separate compilation, and the export of Modelica components encapsulated in a FMU[20]. Currently, this can be done only under the stringent assumption that the input/output orientation of variables appearing at the interface of each compilation unit is fixed, and that the differentiation index is invariant.

Composition of Stochastic Models. Composing stochastic models is a true challenge. Composition operators can be easily defined, under the assumption that the probability laws of the two models are independent. Unfortunately, this assumption most often makes no sense when considering models representing viewpoints of the same component. It turns out that these probability distributions are marginal probabilities of hidden probability distributions defining the stochastic behavior of the component. Marginal probabilities are in general not independent. Several stochastic system theories with good composability properties have been proposed. Unfortunately, their composition operators are involved [3,27,33,41] and none of them have been implemented in a DSL, using the techniques developed in this book.

What Is the Difference Between Compatibility and Consistency? A component model is said to be consistent if it admits at least one correct realization. Since components are often described according to several viewpoints, two models related to the same component are consistent if and only if there exists a common correct realization of both models. Hence, consistency is a logical property that applies to sets of models related to the same component.

Compatibility applies to models related to distinct interacting components. Two models are compatible if and only if there exists an environment of both components such that every realization of the two components can work together. This may have many different meanings. Type compatibility is the simplest form of compatibility. For example, the compatibility of two Interface Automata [39] means that there exists an environment that will prevent the occurrence of an output event whenever the peer component may not be ready to perform the corresponding input. This notion of compatibility appears also in several other specification formalisms, for instance Modal Interfaces [28], Sociable Interfaces [38] and Session Types [30]. Another fine example of compatibility is the Eiffel programming language [4], where preconditions and postconditions attached

---

[19] https://modelica.org.
[20] functional mock-up unit, https://www.fmi-standard.org.

to methods are evaluated at runtime and can raise an exception whenever a component is incorrectly used.

How Do We Check Compatibility and Consistency of a Composition? Consistency and compatibility are semantic properties of the composition of several components that can be checked statically, or by using model-checking techniques, or at runtime, depending on the semantic domains of the involved DSLs. Type-checking and timing constraints are classical examples.

How Can We Exploit Legacy Tools in an Integrated System? Specific domains, such as mechanical engineering or control engineering, each have well-established tool sets that allows users to perform their tasks efficiently. Globalizing DSLs implies that different tools must work together. Therefore the integrated system output from the composition of DSLs must be able to exploit existing tools without modifying them. Although tool integration is not a new problem[21], it is important to re-use and not re-invent tools for specific DSLs. When composing DSLs, their affiliated tools must remain part of the globalization and therefore appropriate interfacing between the different tools must be investigated.

3.2 Collaboration in a Globalized Environment

Overall Consistency Along the Lifecycle of DSL Instances. Models are used to specify and capture different aspects of a system. Although each DSL has a specific purpose, their instance models might need to refer to elements from other models conforming to other DSLs. As such, a model can end up being coupled and inter-related to other models, where it is likely the referenced model is owned by a different stakeholder.

Coordination is required when a model is updated but a given stakeholder might not be aware how a provided model is being used by other parts of the design. There may be few means available to assess the impact that changes may lead to. Furthermore the client stakeholder who is consuming and referencing elements from the other model may have no other choice than to inspect the changes made by the provider to assess their impact on the client model. This leads to a contradiction: both stakeholders, each having different concerns and a dedicated language, have to understand the language of the other stakeholder to collaborate.

In this context coordination requires many interactions among stakeholders who are not even from the same domain. If DSLs can be processed in a unified way, and the language engineer is the most competent person to express requirements between language, shouldn't there be the potential of reducing and managing this coordination at the tool level? Coupling has to be considered as a first-class citizen by the language engineer: in a globalized environment in which

---

[21] Pheonix: http://www.phoenix-int.com/software/phx-modelcenter.php.

language reuse and integration are no longer the exception but the general rule, the language engineer needs to express which concepts are suitable for being referenced or extended (probably among other possible relationships) and these might have an impact at the model level regarding instance evolution.

The challenge is to provide a conceptual framework to the language engineer to extend DSL definitions so that their instances can be coordinated without requiring the different stakeholders to understand all the domains their work is coupled to.

How to Characterize a Change for Stakeholders. Enabling the collaboration of different stakeholders through specific languages at a minimum requires changes to be expressed using a language any stakeholder will understand. Changes either need to have an obvious semantic for each stakeholder, or to be unique so that they can be understood by all stakeholders. Changes are the backbone of collaboration hence have to focus on three properties of socially translucent systems: visibility, awareness, and accountability [20].

How and When Does the Language Engineer Characterize Model Compatibility. In the context of multiple DSLs each having their own semantics we have to ask what is a "compatible" change. Is it a change that preserves the semantics of the model? Is it a change that preserves the fact that all model instances that were visible are still visible? Just going through several examples of DSLs it appears that there might be different aspects exposed by a DSL, each of them probably having its own notion of "compatibility".

In the SERS use case, autonomous vehicles are represented in the system in the form of a Computer Aided Design (CAD) model, parts of which are referred to by other models: the SmartIntersection model refers to a vehicle's position, while Mission Command & Control use the longevity and payload characterizations of the CAD model to reach control decisions.

When a CAD model evolves in reaction to a change in the vehicle's design or characteristics, it is very likely that decisions captured in other models need to be revised. On the other hand many evolutions of the CAD model will have no effect whatsoever on the other models. Since the CAD model provides different aspects, changes made in the CAD models might impact those aspects in a compatible or incompatible way, and consumers will need to assess this impact.

Furthermore in the context of a global collaborative process one has to ask when compatibility should be checked, and when consumers of models should be notified of incompatibilities. This can have a dramatic effect on the collaborative process: too late and much work will need to be done by the other stakeholders, too frequent and the stakeholders will use most of their time to align their work with the other changes. There is a need to be isolated yet informed; in this balance resides a key factor of collaborative process efficiency.

How Should the Concrete Syntax Be Impacted by the Use of an External Language? The concrete DSL syntax is the primary means available to stakeholders to adapt and change the models. When parts of models are in semantic relationships with other elements from an external language, new aspects are mandatory to achieve a seamless use of multiple DSLs: concrete syntaxes have to be integrated (See the Syntactic Integration Sect. 2.3), and navigation between the syntaxes has to be considered a first class citizen.

How do we define a concrete syntax so that parts of it can be reused or merged with others, especially when the types referred to in the languages differ? We will might need to embed parts of a textual syntax into another textual language, or possible into a graphical language. What is the common ground to achieve these syntactic integrations?

Besides these questions, in an open world DSLs and their concrete syntaxes are not known beforehand and as such these issues should be adressed without any specific operation by the end-user. The challenge is that the role of a tool integrator doesn't exist in such context and the DSL and concrete syntax definitions themselves will have to be adapted so that the environment can provide such services at runtime.

Multi-view Modeling Shared by Multiple Stakeholders. The collaboration between stakeholders requires an appropriate tool support for sharing and jointly working on common models. There are three possible multi-view modeling scenarios [16]: (1) Stakeholders are working on exactly the same artifact: both of them share the same screen. All changes made by one stakeholder are directly reflected and perceived by the other stakeholders, such as in Google Docs. This situation is useful when, for example, two stakeholders are manually inspecting a model together, if one stakeholder is training the other, or in a development process favoring pair development. In this case, the collaboration is performed at the granularity of individual model elements and conflicting operations are resolved per element (or group of elements) as done in AToMPM [46]. (2) Stakeholders are working on different viewpoints of the same model. This situation is useful when artifacts are designed incrementally. This is possible when the language in which the artifact is described, offers a modularity mechanism that allows one to split its instances into different parts, such as partial classes in C# and aliases in UML diagrams. In this case, each viewpoint evolves separately, and changes are made locally to each viewpoint. At specific moments (on save or commit), changes from different viewpoints are merged into the underlying model. Conflicts that arise must then be resolved one by one by an expert as in WebGME. (3) Stakeholders with differing expertise are working on distinct models that, together, compose the overall system. Each artifact represents a concern of the overall system, e.g., the electrical, software, and the security concerns of an automotive. This is useful when a system is designed by separating its concerns, such as in aspect-oriented programming. This case requires traceability across DSLs. The traces need to be modeled explicitly in order to specify, at the language level, how conflicts are resolved automatically at the model level as in eMoflon [35].

Large Scale Model Management. A collaborative modeling environment typically requires more storage space and more efficient model manipulation techniques than in a single-user modeling environment. Models grow in size more rapidly because multiple stakeholders are contributing and evolving them. Furthermore, traceability links between viewpoints, models, and DSLs must be stored. It is therefore of paramount importance to seek a suitable data model for persistent storage. Typically, all modeling artifacts are stored centrally on a distributed cloud server. Graph databases are of particular interest because they are optimized for graph representations of models as opposed to relational SQL database that have been shown to not perform as well [50]. Example candidates are: Neo4j which supports transaction processing [2], Trinity which virtualizes random-access memory of a cluster of computer nodes [6], and Apache Giraph which relies on the Hadoop paradigm [32]. A starting point for comparison is Shah *et al.*'s tool for benchmarking NoSQL databases to store models [44].

4   Conclusion

After presenting an overview of current work related to the composition of tools, models and languages, this chapter compiled a list of key open challenges related to both technical coordination of domain-specific languages and to social coordination of stakeholders in a globalized environment. While many challenges have to be addressed before achieving the globalization of modeling languages, the number of recent works that are currently paving the road toward this globalization makes these challenges very exciting.

References

1. Alam, O., Kienzle, J., Mussbacher, G.: Concern-oriented software design. In: Moreira, A., Schätz, B., Gray, J., Vallecillo, A., Clarke, P. (eds.) MODELS 2013. LNCS, vol. 8107, pp. 604–621. Springer, Heidelberg (2013)
2. Benelallam, A., Gómez, A., Sunyé, G., Tisi, M., Launay, D.: Neo4EMF, a scalable persistence layer for EMF models. In: Cabot, J., Rubin, J. (eds.) ECMFA 2014. LNCS, vol. 8569, pp. 230–241. Springer, Heidelberg (2014)
3. Caillaud, B., Delahaye, B., Larsen, K.G., Legay, A., Pedersen, M.L., Wasowski, A.: Constraint markov chains. Theor. Comput. Sci. **412**(34), 4373–4404 (2011)
4. Meyer, B.: Eiffel: The Language. Prentice-Hall, Upper Saddle River (1991)
5. Bézivin, J., Brunelière, H., Cabot, J., Doux, G., Jouault, F., Sottet, J.-S., et al.: Model driven tool interoperability in practice. In: Proceedings of the 3rd Workshop on Model-Driven Tool & Process Integration (co-located with ECMFA 2010), pp. 62–72 (2010)
6. Shao, B., Wang, H., Li, Y.: The Trinity Graph Engine. Technical report MSR-TR-2012-30, March 2012
7. Blochwitz, T., Otter, M., Arnold, M., Bausch, C., Clauß, C., Elmqvist, H., Junghanns, A., Mauss, J., Monteiro, M., Neidhold, T., et al.: The functional mockup interface for tool independent exchange of simulation models. In: 8th International Modelica Conference, Dresden, pp. 20–22 (2011)

8. Broman, D., Siek, J.G.: Modelyze: a Gradually Typed Host Language for Embedding Equation-Based Modeling Languages. Technical report UCB/EECS-2012-173, EECS Department, University of California, Berkeley, Jun 2012
9. Ford, B.: Parsing expression grammars: a recognition-based syntactic foundation. In: POPL 2004: Proceedings of the 31st ACM SIGPLAN-SIGACT Symposium on Principles of Programming Languages, pp. 111–122. ACM, New York (2004)
10. Burmester, S., Giese, H., Niere, J., Tichy, M., Wadsack, J.P., Wagner, R., Wendehals, L., Zündorf, A.: Tool integration at the meta-model level: the Fujaba approach. Int. J. Softw. Tools Technol. Transf. **6**(3), 203–218 (2004)
11. Caracciolo, A., Lungu, M., Nierstrasz, O.: A unified approach to architecture conformance checking. In: Proceedings of the 12th Working IEEE/IFIP Conference on Software Architecture (WICSA). ACM Press (2015)
12. Carriero, N., Gelernter, D.: How to write parallel programs: a guide to the perplexed. ACM Comput. Surv. **21**(3), 323–357 (1989)
13. Clavreul, M.: Model and Metamodel Composition: Separation of Mapping and Interpretation for Unifying Existing Model Composition Techniques. Ph.D. thesis, Université Rennes 1 (2011)
14. Combemale, B., De Antoni, J., Larsen, M.V., Mallet, F., Barais, O., Baudry, B., France, R.B.: Reifying concurrency for executable metamodeling. In: Erwig, M., Paige, R.F., Van Wyk, E. (eds.) SLE 2013. LNCS, vol. 8225, pp. 365–384. Springer, Heidelberg (2013)
15. Cordy, J.R.: The TXL source transformation language. Sci. Comput. Program. **61**(3), 190–210 (2006)
16. Corley, J., Ergin, H., Van Mierlo, S., Syriani, E.: Cloud-based multi-view modeling environments. In: Modern Software Engineering Methodologies for Mobile and Cloud Environments. IGI Global (2015)
17. Broman, D., Brooks, C.X., Greenberg, L., Lee, E.A., Masin, M., Tripakis, S., Wetter, M.: Determinate composition of FMUs for co-simulation. In: Proceedings of the International Conference on Embedded Software, EMSOFT 2013, Montreal, QC, Canada, September 29–October 4, 2013, pp. 1–12. IEEE (2013)
18. Eker, J., Janneck, J.W., Lee, E.A., Liu, J., Liu, X., Ludvig, J., Neuendorffer, S., Sachs, S., Xiong, Y.: Taming heterogeneity - the Ptolemy approach. Proc. IEEE **91**(1), 127–144 (2003)
19. Erdweg, S., Giarrusso, P.G., Rendel, T.: Language composition untangled. In: Proceedings of the Twelfth Workshop on Language Descriptions, Tools, and Applications, LDTA 2012, pp. 7:1–7:8. ACM, New York (2012)
20. Erickson, T., Kellogg, W.A.: Social translucence: an approach to designing systems that support social processes. ACM Trans. Comput. Hum. Interact. **7**(1), 59–83 (2000)
21. Jackson, E.K., Kang, E., Dahlweid, M., Seifert, D., Santen, T.: Components, platforms and possibilities: towards generic automation for MDA. In: EMSOFT, pp. 39–48. ACM (2010)
22. Fowler, M.: Language Workbenches: The Killer-App for Domain-Specific Languages, June 2005
23. Baader, F., Nipkow, T.: Term Rewriting and All That. Cambridge University Press, Cambridge (1998)
24. Frost, R., Launchbury, J.: Constructing natural language interpreters in a lazy functional language. Comput. J. **32**(2), 108–121 (1989)
25. Papadopoulos, G.A., Arbab, F.: Coordination Models and Languages. Advances in Computers, vol. 46, pp. 329–400. Elsevier, Amsterdam (1998)

26. Hardebolle, C., Boulanger, F.: ModHel'X: a component-oriented approach to multi-formalism modeling. In: Giese, H. (ed.) MODELS 2008. LNCS, vol. 5002, pp. 247–258. Springer, Heidelberg (2008)

27. Kozine, I., Utkin, L.V.: Interval-valued finite markov chains. Reliable Comput. **8**(2), 97–113 (2002)

28. Raclet, J.-B., Badouel, E., Benveniste, A., Caillaud, B., Legay, A., Passerone, R.: A modal interface theory for component-based design. Fundam. Inform. **108**(1–2), 119–149 (2011)

29. Karsai, G., Lang, A., Neema, S.: Design patterns for open tool integration. Softw. Syst. Model. **4**(2), 157–170 (2005)

30. Honda, K.: Session types and distributed computing. In: Czumaj, A., Mehlhorn, K., Pitts, A., Wattenhofer, R. (eds.) ICALP 2012, Part II. LNCS, vol. 7392, pp. 23–23. Springer, Heidelberg (2012)

31. Kramler, G., Kappel, G., Reiter, T., Kapsammer, E., Retschitzegger, W., Schwinger, W.: Towards a semantic infrastructure supporting model-based tool integration. In: Proceedings of the 2006 International Workshop on Global Integrated Model Management, pp. 43–46. ACM (2006)

32. Krause, C., Tichy, M., Giese, H.: Implementing graph transformations in the bulk synchronous parallel model. In: Gnesi, S., Rensink, A. (eds.) FASE 2014 (ETAPS). LNCS, vol. 8411, pp. 325–339. Springer, Heidelberg (2014)

33. Chatterjee, K., Sen, K., Henzinger, T.A.: Model-checking ω-regular properties of interval Markov chains. In: Amadio, R.M. (ed.) FOSSACS 2008. LNCS, vol. 4962, pp. 302–317. Springer, Heidelberg (2008)

34. Kuhl, F., Dahmann, J., Weatherly, R.: Creating Computer Simulation Systems: An Introduction to the High Level Architecture. Prentice Hall PTR, Upper Saddle River (2000)

35. Leblebici, E., Anjorin, A., Schürr, A.: Developing eMoflon with eMoflon. In: Di Ruscio, D., Varró, D. (eds.) ICMT 2014. LNCS, vol. 8568, pp. 138–145. Springer, Heidelberg (2014)

36. Ledeczi, A., Volgyesi, P., Karsai, G.: Metamodel composition in the generic modeling environment. In: Communications at Workshop on Adaptive Object-Models and Metamodeling Techniques, Ecoop, vol. 1 (2001)

37. Kats, L.C.L., Visser, E.: The spoofax language workbench. Rules for declarative specification of languages and IDEs. In: Rinard, M. (ed.) Proceedings of the 25th Annual ACM SIGPLAN Conference on Object-Oriented Programming, Systems, Languages, and Applications, OOPSLA 2010, October 17–21, 2010, Reno, NV, USA, pp. 444–463 (2010)

38. de Alfaro, L., da Silva, L.D., Faella, M., Legay, A., Roy, P., Sorea, M.: Sociable interfaces. In: Gramlich, B. (ed.) FroCos 2005. LNCS (LNAI), vol. 3717, pp. 81–105. Springer, Heidelberg (2005)

39. de Alfaro, L., Henzinger, T.A.: Interface automata. In: Proceedings of the 9th ACM SIGSOFT International Symposium on Foundations of Software Engineering (FSE'01), pp. 109–120. ACM Press (2001)

40. Renggli, L., Gîrba, T., Nierstrasz, O.: Embedding languages without breaking tools. In: D'Hondt, T. (ed.) ECOOP 2010. LNCS, vol. 6183, pp. 380–404. Springer, Heidelberg (2010)

41. Abbes, S., Benveniste, A.: True-concurrency probabilistic models: Markov nets and a law of large numbers. Theor. Comput. Sci. **390**(2–3), 129–170 (2008)

42. Sander, I., Jantsch, A.: System modeling and transformational design refinement in ForSyDe [formal system design]. IEEE Trans. Comput. Aided Des. Integr. Circ. Syst. **23**(1), 17–32 (2004)

43. Scott, E., Johnstone, A.: GLL Parsing. Electron. Notes Theor. Comput. Sci. **253**(7), 177–189 (2010)
44. Shah, S.M., Wei, R., Kolovos, D.S., Rose, L.M., Paige, R.F., Barmpis, K.: A framework to benchmark NoSQL data stores for large-scale model persistence. In: Dingel, J., Schulte, W., Ramos, I., Abrahão, S., Insfran, E. (eds.) MODELS 2014. LNCS, vol. 8767, pp. 586–601. Springer, Heidelberg (2014)
45. Steinberg, D., Budinsky, F., Paternostro, M., Merks, E.: EMF: Eclipse Modeling Framework 2.0. Addison-Wesley Professional, Reading (2009)
46. Syriani, E., Vangheluwe, H., Mannadiar, R., Hansen, C., Van Mierlo, S., Ergin, H.: AToMPM: a web-based modeling environment. In: MODELS 2013: Invited Talks, Demos, Posters, and ACM SRC, vol. 1115. CEUR-WS.org, Miami (2013)
47. Sztipanovits, J., Bapty, T., Neema, S., Howard, L., Jackson, E.: OpenMETA: a model- and component-based design tool chain for cyber-physical systems. In: Bensalem, S., Lakhneck, Y., Legay, A. (eds.) From Programs to Systems. LNCS, vol. 8415, pp. 235–248. Springer, Heidelberg (2014)
48. Tomita, M.: Efficient Parsing for Natural Language: A Fast Algorithm for Practical Systems, vol. 8. Springer, New York (1985)
49. Larsen, M.E.V., Deantoni, J., Combemale, B., Mallet, F.: A behavioral coordination operator language (BCOoL). In: ACM/IEEE 18th International Conference on Model Driven Engineering Languages and Systems (Models) (2015)
50. Varró, G., Friedl, K., Varró, D.: Implementing a graph transformation engine in relational databases. J. Softw. Syst. Model. **5**(3), 313–341 (2006)
51. White, J., Odeh, F., Sangiovanni Vincentelli, A.L., Ruehli, A.: Waveform relaxation: theory and practice. Technical report UCB/ERL M85/65, EECS Department, University of California, Berkeley (1985)

Author Index

Printed in the United States
By Bookmasters